DINOSAURS TO DRAGONS

THE LORE AND SCIENCE OF MYTHICAL CREATURES

ELIZABETH SHREEVE

ILLUSTRATED BY
VIOLETA ENCARNACIÓN

Atheneum Books for Young Readers
NEW YORK · AMSTERDAM/ANTWERP · LONDON
TORONTO · SYDNEY/MELBOURNE · NEW DELHI

DINOSAURS
DINOSAURS
DINOSAURS
DINOSAURS
DINOSAURS
DINOSAURS
DRAGONS
DRAGONS
DRAGONS
DRAGONS

For Sophie, who might just be a mermaid.
Te amo mucho, Nana.
—E. S.

For Victor — dinosaur expert and biology genius —
for showing me that science has its own kind of magic.
—V. E.

ATHENEUM BOOKS FOR YOUNG READERS · An imprint of Simon & Schuster Children's Publishing Division · 1230 Avenue of the Americas, New York, New York 10020 · For more than 100 years, Simon & Schuster has championed authors and the stories they create. By respecting the copyright of an author's intellectual property, you enable Simon & Schuster and the author to continue publishing exceptional books for years to come. We thank you for supporting the author's copyright by purchasing an authorized edition of this book. · For information about special discounts for bulk purchases, please contact Simon & Schuster Special Sales at 1-866-506-1949 or business@simonandschuster.com. · Simon & Schuster strongly believes in freedom of expression and stands against censorship in all its forms. For more information, visit BooksBelong.com. · The Simon & Schuster Speakers Bureau can bring authors to your live event. For more information or to book an event, contact the Simon & Schuster Speakers Bureau at 1-866-248-3049 or visit our website at www.simonspeakers.com. · The text for this book was set in Silva Text. · The illustrations for this book were rendered digitally. · Manufactured in Malaysia · 0326 SCP · First Edition · 10 9 8 7 6 5 4 3 2 1 · CIP data for this book is available from the Library of Congress. · ISBN 9781665941006 · ISBN 9781665941020 (ebook)

Please note: The standard typographical rule is to set the scientific names of creatures (genus and species) in italics. In certain instances, scientific names have instead been set in boldface for ease of legibility.

CONTENTS

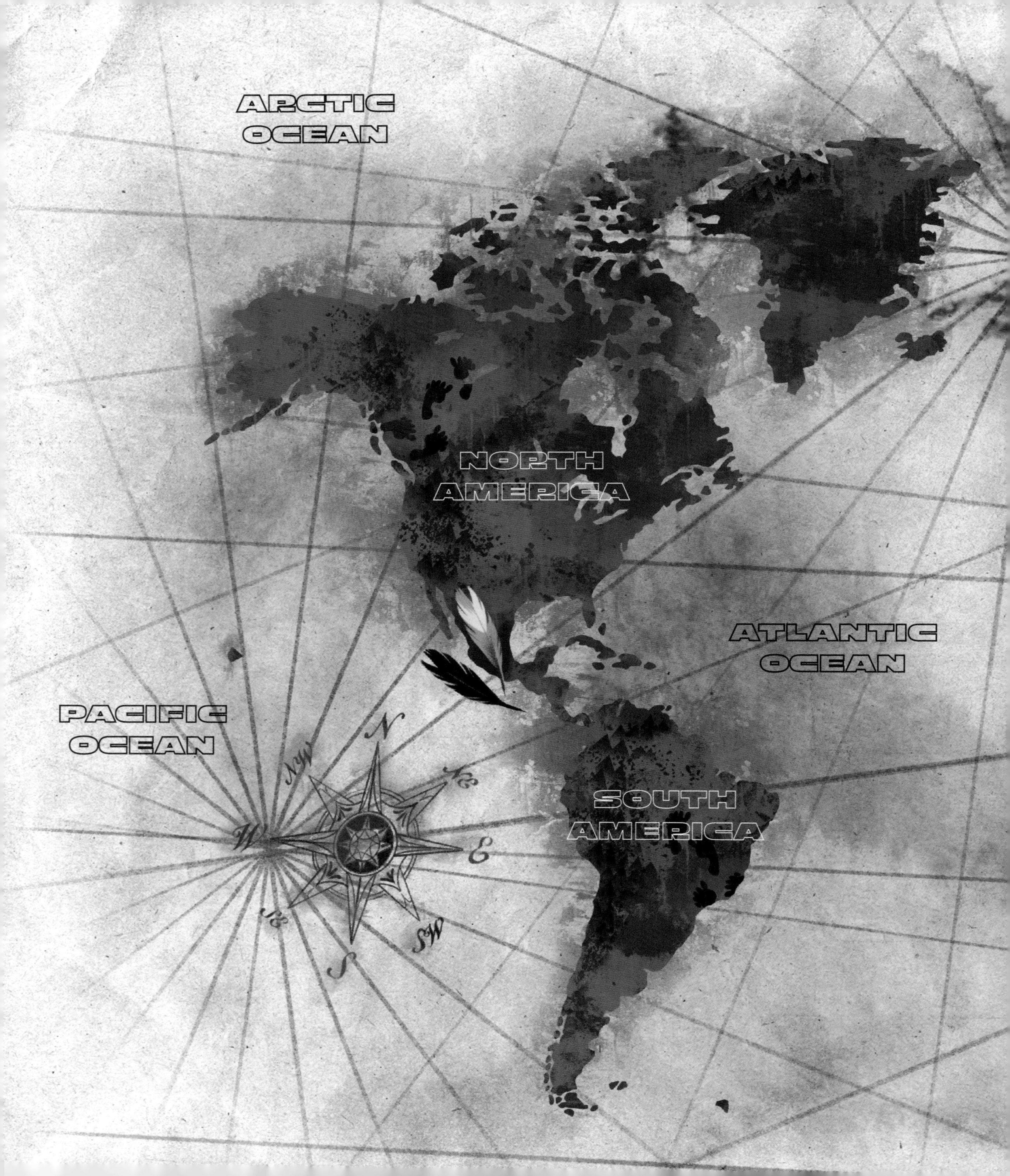

ARCTIC
OCEAN

NORTH
AMERICA

ATLANTIC
OCEAN

PACIFIC
OCEAN

SOUTH
AMERICA

ARCTIC OCEAN
EUROPE
ASIA
AFRICA
PACIFIC OCEAN
INDIAN OCEAN
AUSTRALIA

IN THE DEEP
LONG AGO . . .

Before we understood the origins and vast timeline of life on Earth . . .

Our ancestors found strange bones in the dirt. Skeletons that seemed to combine features of birds and beasts. Enormous skulls with what looked like one huge eye socket instead of two smaller ones. Thigh bones taller than a man. Teeth as long as daggers.

Could these be the bones of vanished giants? Evidence of mythical monsters or the remains of heroes, left from long-ago wars?

People glimpsed living animals, too, that they could not explain. What exactly were those sea beasts, half hidden in fog? And the broad-winged creatures high in the sky, with the magical power of flight . . . were they messengers from the heavens? What dangers did they pose?

To make sense of these mysteries, people spun stories of wondrous beings. Tales unfolded through time. Monsters grew bigger, faster, more powerful. In all corners of the world, legends of bizarre animals came alive in poems, paintings, and songs. Stories of long-tentacled sea monsters. Flags adorned with sharp-clawed predators. Paintings of splendid birds born from nests of blazing fire.

Today we understand far more about the world and its creatures. Yet many myths live on, spurring fear and delight in books, movies, artwork, games, and more.

Where and when did those stories first begin? No one can say for sure. But in these pages, we'll imagine moments when myths of ten fabulous beings might have taken shape. Together these creatures represent the realms of land, water, and air. Some are famous, like dragons and mermaids. Others may be less familiar, inviting explorations into new territory. We'll crisscross the globe to discover their tales. We'll visit the cultures and landscapes where they emerged. And using the tools of science, we'll ask: Could there be grains of truth at the hearts of these legends?

GRIFFIN
Guardian of Gold

LET'S IMAGINE . . .

A Scythian horsewoman gallops through the desert hills of central Asia almost three thousand years ago. The wind howls. Rocky cliffs glow red and orange in the morning sun, rising against jagged, snowy peaks on the horizon.

Near the ridgetop, a landslide blocks the trail. The rider reins in her horse and scans the terrain, searching for another route. Far to the west she sees a caravan of covered wagons moving through a dry, grassy valley. Are they enemies or friends? She touches the bow and quiver of arrows that hang from her belt. These mountains hold a secret of her people — precious gold, found in places known only to a few. Gold that sometimes draws unwanted strangers.

Wind tears the clouds apart, sending a pattern of sunlight and shadows sweeping across the hills. In one swift movement, the woman dismounts. The fallen rocks have revealed shapes in the cliff face: a skull with a beaked nose, like a giant bird of prey, and a jaw packed with teeth. She pushes loose rubble aside and finds other bones captured in stone — legs, ribs, and shoulders, heavy and strong. She picks a crooked-fingered claw from the debris, but it crumbles in her grip.

What could this creature have been?

From the elders she's heard rumors of a fierce, wolf-sized animal in these hills. Here is proof, laid bare by a landslide. If this creature were alive, she would train it as she did her sturdy horse. It would help to protect her family's treasure.

When she returns home, the horsewoman has a story to share of what she's seen. The story of a bird-monster, with the head and claws of an eagle and the body of a lion.

Fierce guardian of gold —

the griffin.

THE SCYTHIANS

If you had a treasure, would you conjure up a terrifying creature to protect it?

The scene of the horsewoman is an invented one, informed by what we know about the Scythians — ancient nomads who roamed much of central Asia from around 900 BCE to 300 CE. Scythian culture included many different tribal groups linked by lifestyles centered on horse riding, archery, and warfare. Armed with powerful short bows, pointed battle-axes, and arrows smeared with snake venom, the Scythians defended themselves against some of the ancient world's greatest conquerors, including the powerful Persian king known as Darius the Great.

Scythian tribes inhabited the vast cold, dry grasslands known as the Eurasian steppes. This was a landscape of movement, perfectly suited to life on horseback. Boys and girls alike learned to ride, hunt, and shoot while at full gallop, controlling their horses with knees and calves. Some historians suggest that the skill of Scythian horse riders gave rise to another mythical animal — the centaur, a horselike creature that was human from the waist up.

In addition to hunting and raiding, some Scythian tribes mined for gold in the eastern regions beyond the Altai Mountains. Today this area straddles the countries of Kazakhstan, Russia, Mongolia, and China. Long ago, in an uncharted landscape, hardy nomads crafted beautiful gold armor, cups, and jewelry decorated with wild beasts that they observed or imagined — including griffins.

Fierce and Swift

The Scythian nomads were expert horse riders, archers, and masters of hit-and-run battle tactics.

Treasures of Gold

The Scythians were known for remarkable metalwork as well as equestrian skills. This griffin ornament dates from the fifth century BCE, a full 2,500 years ago. Other treasures depict animals from nature and warriors in battle.

LEGENDS AND LORE

Enemies beware!

With an eagle's piercing scream and a lion's graceful strength, the griffin lopes through time, reappearing in many places and tales. Early illustrations of hybrid bird-mammals date back to 3300 BCE, in Egypt and Mesopotamia, the historical region of West Asia located between the Tigris and Euphrates Rivers. But the first known written account of griffins comes from a poem about Scythia by a Greek traveler named Aristeas around 675 BCE — some 2,700 years ago.

Around that time, Scythian nomads began trading with the Greeks, whose influence extended beyond the Mediterranean region to West Asia. Scythians did not have a written language, but the Greeks eagerly recorded their stories. One tale told of the mighty griffin — a half-eagle, half-lion beast — that guarded treasures of gold in the Altai Mountains. These wild animals were said to lay eggs in burrows on the ground, which they defended with vicious claws and sharp beaks. The Greek historian Herodotus wrote of the Arimaspians, a mythical race of one-eyed people who tried to steal gold nuggets from griffin nests.

As trade expanded, the griffin legend spread westward. The creature grew more impressive through time. By the Middle Ages, between roughly 500 and 1500 CE, a griffin was said to be larger than eight lions. It carried the force of a hundred eagles — enough to lift a horse and rider in its claws — and laid eggs studded with jewels. Related creatures emerged, like the hippogriff, a cross between a griffin and a horse. On medieval armor and flags, griffins stood for royalty, strength, and protection — or sometimes the cruelty and greed of the noble class.

Yet even as the reputation of griffins became more fantastical, travelers were exploring and mapping the world. Around 1250, a learned German philosopher named Albertus Magnus realized that no one had, well, actually seen a griffin. The stories were simply . . . stories! In Lewis Carroll's *Alice's Adventures in Wonderland*, the famous novel of 1865, a griffin (or "gryphon," as Carroll spelled it) lies asleep in the sun — no longer frightening or dangerous, but a bit lazy and prone to hiccups. Despite its fierce nature, the griffin had become the stuff of children's stories.

Today we see griffins as logos for banks, schools, cities, and sports teams. Griffins still leap through the stories and imagery of magical tales, but they live only in legends. Which leaves a question: What were those mysterious bones in the rocky cliffs beyond the Altai Mountains?

Now the place where the griffins live and the gold is found is a grim and terrible desert. Waiting for a moonless night, the treasure-seekers come with shovels and sacks and dig. If they manage to elude the griffins, the men reap a double reward, for they escape with their lives and bring home a cargo of gold — rich profit for the dangers they face.

—Roman author Aelian, c. 200 CE

Powers of Two Predators

The griffin combines features of two powerful predators: the eagle and the lion. It's an example of a chimera—a mythical creature with parts taken from various animals. (Keep your eyes out for more chimeras later in the book.) Despite having wings, griffins are usually depicted as land-dwelling animals. The word **grypòs** comes from an ancient Greek word meaning "hooked," like a raptor's beak. In 1662 a Czech artist depicted this griffin at home in the European landscape, surrounded by plants and fruits.

Alexander's Griffins

According to a Byzantine medieval legend, griffins attacked the army of Alexander the Great during his campaign into India. Alexander turned this to his advantage by attaching some of the beasts to a chariot and traveling through the sky. To entice the great bird-monsters, he held skewers of meat above their heads. Fly, fly!

TRACKING DOWN CLUES

In the 1920s, the American Museum of Natural History sponsored the Central Asiatic Expeditions into the Gobi Desert in hopes of uncovering secrets of the prehistoric past. Explorers of the era had heard Chinese folklore about dragon bones and teeth. Other reports told of giant "bird-monsters." The expedition, led by Roy Chapman Andrews, would bring a team of American, Chinese, and Mongolian workers to explore the lands where Scythian nomads had once roamed.

In most places, fossils are difficult to find. The expeditioners faced the possibility of failure along with the dangers of sandstorms, snakes, and bandit attacks. But as they journeyed west in the Gobi Desert, the team discovered a landscape of windblown rock layers strewn with skeletons of dinosaurs, including many species that were new to science. At a site called Bayn Dzak — also known as the Flaming Cliffs — they collected over one ton of fossils, including full-grown dinosaurs with enormous claws, babies, and clutches of eggs. White bones poked out of crumbly reddish sediments. The most common fossil was that of a wolf-sized animal with a frill of bone at its neck, long birdlike shoulder blades, and a hooked beak — the dinosaur they named *Protoceratops*, or "first horned face." These animals thrived in central Asia around eighty to seventy-five million years ago.

More recently a historian named Adrienne Mayor noticed the similarities between *Protoceratops* fossils and the legendary griffin. Both creatures appeared to combine features of birds and mammals. It's easy to imagine, she suggested, that someone long ago could envision the hatchet-shaped face of the beaked *Protoceratops* as that of a huge eagle. Likewise, the dinosaur's shoulder bones or neck frill could suggest wings. Possible outcome? The griffin — a mythical creature much scarier than the plant-eating beaked dinosaur of the distant past.

Political strife put an end to the Central Asiatic Expeditions in 1930, but later expeditions returned. A joint team of Mongolian and Polish paleontologists discovered more fossils in the 1960s. In 1990, scientists from the Mongolian Academy of Sciences began a joint program with the American Museum of Natural History in the Gobi Desert. Their many discoveries help us to understand the lives of dinosaurs, many of which were as fast-moving and energetic as their modern-day relatives — birds. Not so different, it turns out, from the way ancient people once imagined the lives of griffins.

Bird-Monsters of the Gobi

This painting, created by Robert J. Barber for the American Museum of Natural History, shows **Protoceratops** among **Velociraptor** and other dinosaurs that inhabited Mongolia around seventy-two million years ago.

Dinosaur with a Beak

Protoceratops andrewsi likely grazed in large herds, doing their best to avoid becoming lunch for larger animals. Based on fossil discoveries, we know that they laid eggs in nests on the ground. The bony neck frills may have provided protection from predators. These six-foot-long dinosaurs were ancient cousins of the **Triceratops** dinosaurs of North America.

Stories of fabulous creatures can arise from the human imagination without any physical evidence — but fossils have certainly influenced ancient and medieval lore and images of mythical animals.

—Adrienne Mayor, historian of folklore and ancient science

TO BE A GRIFFIN

What would it take for a griffin to be a real, living animal? Throughout the book, this section will consider scientific aspects of mythical creatures. Some of them may be more likely to dwell in legends than the real world, but each one has plenty to reveal about how animals evolve and thrive.

For griffins, let's start by considering the wings. To achieve powered flight, animals must defy gravity in two ways: They need to launch from the ground and then stay airborne. An animal's weight is a major constraint — and a medium-sized male lion weighs around four hundred pounds. Based on the typical weight-to-wingspan ratio of birds, a flying lion would need an enormous wingspan. Those giant wings would make it difficult to clear the ground and start flapping.

Good news for griffins — cats are great jumpers! Cougars, for example, can jump twenty feet straight into the air. Unfortunately, there's a fatal flaw. Even if a griffin could jump high enough to flap once or twice . . . *boom!* They'd come straight back down. A lion's body is adapted to the rough-and-tumble life of a land-dwelling predator. Their thick skulls can withstand a zebra's kick, and their powerful limbs provide speed and strength for knocking down prey. But they're heavy, and also lack the strong breastbones and chest muscles of flying animals.

Okay, maybe griffin wings were only for show? After all, the creatures are usually depicted on the ground. Here we run into a problem from way back in time. Around four hundred million years ago certain types of fish evolved into what we call tetrapods — four-limbed animals with backbones. Reptiles, amphibians, mammals, and birds all have four limbs. A bird's wings are simply the elongated, feather-covered arms of its ground-dwelling dinosaur ancestors. Some creatures, such as snakes, have lost their limbs. Despite the many variations, however, tetrapods never have more than four.

But griffins have six limbs — four legs and two wings. From a biological perspective, that's hard to swallow. There are, of course, plenty of six-legged critters. They're the most numerous and diverse animals on Earth.

We call them . . . insects. And not a single one of them could ever pass as a griffin.

A griffin from Egypt during Roman rule, in the second century CE.

A dragon and griffin battle in this illustration from the seventeenth century.

A marble carving from around 350 BCE depicts Amazons and Greeks in battle.

Siberian Ice Maiden

You've probably heard that tattoos will last your whole life—or in the case of the Siberian Ice Maiden, more like 2,400 years and counting. The Ice Maiden's mummified remains were uncovered in 1993 by Russian archaeologist Dr. Natalia Polosmak and her team. They found a young woman dressed in silk and buried with horses and jewelry. Animal images decorated her tall headdress. The absence of weapons suggests that the Ice Maiden was not a warrior. But on her left shoulder she wore the tattoo of a mythical hybrid creature—a deer with elaborate antlers and a hooked beak.

THE REAL AMAZONS

Griffins belong to the world of myths, but the Scythians gave rise to another legend that proves true. Through the work of archaeologists, the fierce and famous women warriors known as Amazons can now be traced to the lives of Scythian horsewomen.

Scythians left behind burial mounds that dot the grassy steppes from the Black Sea to Mongolia. In some, archaeologists have found spectacular gold weaponry alongside mummified remains from 2,500 years ago, many of whom were women. Approximately one out of three women of the steppes was buried with her bows and arrows, spears, daggers, and horses — and with battle scars that tell of a rugged life of warfare on horseback.

Scythians recorded their lives in another way — with tattoos. Many of the mummies were inscribed with vivid, stylized images of stags, snakes, rams, birds, and fantastical creatures like griffins. Infrared camera technology has revealed detailed tattoos from remains found near the Altai Mountains, where hardy nomads once mined for gold.

No one knows exactly when or where the legend of griffins began. Long ago, traders passing through central Asia may have told stories of eagle-headed lions. Scythian nomads would see bones matching those descriptions. Perhaps these stories and observations combined into the myth of a terrifying predator — a creature that has symbolized power and protection for thousands of years.

Our next mythical animal is equally famous, but a good deal gentler . . . at least most of the time.

UNICORN
Magical and Rare

LET'S IMAGINE . . .

A caravan of traders moves across a swampy grassland in northern India, some 2,500 years ago. Their weary camels plod along, loaded with black polished pottery, sandalwood, spices, and dyes. In the distance the jagged peaks of the Himalayan Mountains fade into clouds.

At the end of the procession a twelve-year-old boy struggles through the thick mud.

"Come along, faster!" calls the cook. "Do you want to be a tiger's dinner?"

The boy starts to run — then freezes as a huge animal bursts from the tall grass. Steam rises from its massive head. A single jutting horn points toward the setting sun. The massive beast turns and charges toward the boy, who staggers backward and falls.

At the last moment the animal veers off and melts into the shadows.

The boy scrambles to his feet and hurries to catch up with his team.

That night, over tea, the men share tales of the far-off court of the Persian king. A place of riches, so they've heard, where money flows like water. It's said that some fools at the court will even part with coins in exchange for stories. The stranger the story, the better.

The image of the horned creature flashes in the boy's mind. An idea takes seed.

In the months and years that follow, the boy joins one caravan after another. He climbs icy peaks. He fends off thirst in the desert. He survives bandits who leave him with nothing but the stories he collects on each journey. The tales grow in his mind through the long, tedious hours of travel, the packing and unpacking and feeding of camels. Sometimes they earn him a place by the fire or a second bowlful of stew.

Years later the young man finally reaches the royal court of Persia. There he spins tales of talking birds that sparkle like gems. Men with the heads of dogs. Fountains flowing with liquid gold. And a redheaded, blue-eyed beast with a single magical horn —

the unicorn.

THE SILK ROAD

Legends of mythical creatures like the unicorn date back to ancient times, long before the internet or even printed books. How did these stories spread?

Hint: Ever hear of the Silk Road? This vast collection of caravan tracks extended from China in the east to Italy in the west. The network grew from small pathways to three major routes leading westward from China — a northern one to the Black Sea, a central one to Persia and the Mediterranean Sea, and a southern set of tracks to Afghanistan, Iran, and India. For over two thousand years, traders led long lines of camels along these trails, crossing high mountains, treacherous marshes, and scorching deserts to bring their wares to market. Precious silks came from China along with gemstones, teas, and ceramics. Middle Eastern merchants brought ivory, glass, spices, and finely crafted metal vessels. From Europe came horses, fabrics, and manufactured goods.

Along with these cargoes, travelers on the Silk Road spread ideas and information about art, music, science, and religion. They exchanged stories, too. Legends that told of mighty heroes and gods. Fables that delivered lessons about the consequences of good or foolish behavior. And accounts of wild animals, both imagined and real.

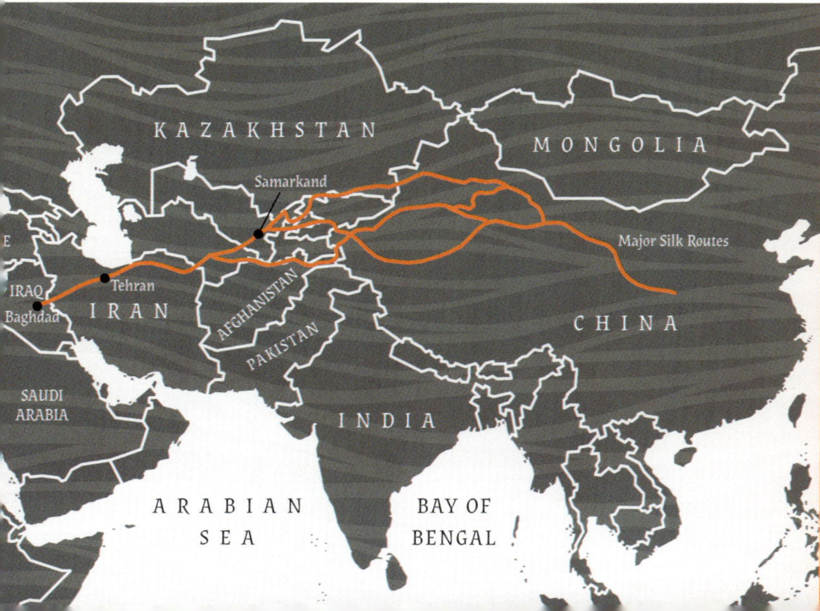

A caravan on the Silk Road, from an atlas of the 1300s.

Ships of the Desert

Camels proved essential for transporting goods on the Silk Road. As captured in this ancient figurine from China dated around 850 CE, the "ships of the desert" carried heavy loads through barren and harsh expanses of Eurasia. Along with commercial goods came the exchange of ideas and information along a network of oasis trading posts.

LEGENDS AND LORE

Quick — imagine a unicorn!

You're probably envisioning an elegant white horse with a spiraling horn, right? It shimmers into view long enough to nibble a slice of watermelon, fart a sparkling cloud of rainbows, and disappear back into its enchanted woodland like the fragment of a dream. Mysterious and beautiful, noble and shy . . .

But wait. Weren't we just reading about a boy who encounters a massive mud-covered rhinoceros?

The unicorn of Western tradition has taken on a wide range of forms and shapes through time. Early descriptions of unicorns date back to around 400 BCE, when a Greek physician named Ctesias served at the court of the Persian king. Ctesias probably never traveled east of Persia, but that didn't stop him from collecting lots of fantastical stories into his book entitled *Indica*, which cataloged stories from the faraway lands of India. Among other animals, *Indica* mentions a swift, powerful animal with a multicolored horn of white, red, and black.

The Greek philosopher Aristotle accepted this account (while grumbling about Ctesias's tendency to exaggerate), and the unicorn became part of a long list of exotic but real animals of the classical world. Then a century later, everything changed. Jewish scholars translating the Bible from Hebrew into Greek found references to a powerful animal called the *re'em*. The original Hebrew word means "beast with a horn" and likely referred to some kind of large cattle or wild ox — but the scholars chose the Greek word *monokeros*, or "one-horn" for their translation. In 1611, when Greek texts were translated into English, the word became "unicorn" instead.

Instant superpowers! The unicorn, now officially added to the popular King James Bible, was celebrated in sculpture, paintings, and manuscripts. Fierce enemy of elephants and lions, the unicorn symbolized purity and strength. Its horn could cure disease, avert poisonings, and purify water with a simple touch. It featured in enormous medieval tapestries, such as the famous series depicting the Hunt of the Unicorn on display at the Met Cloisters Museum in New York City. People liked the idea of the rare, solitary, and untamable creature, though no one had actually seen one.

The popularity of unicorns continued to grow. Today they gallop through movies and games. They decorate clothing, coloring books, pillows, backpacks, and all sorts of toys. We collect them, comb their manes, and dream of finding our own special unicorn, glorious and elusive and certain to bring good luck.

Could they possibly be real?

There are in India certain wild asses which are as large as horses, and larger. Their bodies are white, their heads dark red, and their eyes dark blue. They have a horn on the forehead which is about a foot and a half in length. The dust filed from this horn is administered in a potion as a protection against poisons.

—Ctesias, **Indica**

Changing Shapes

The unicorn took on many shapes and personas over time, as stories spread between different cultures and across vast distances.

An early unicorn-like bull from Pakistan.

The fierce Karkadann of Persia and northern India. Karkadann also means "rhinoceros" in Persian and Arabic.

The virtuous kirin of Japan, known for punishing the wicked, with its single backswept horn.

The qilin of China, a creature so tenderhearted that it avoided stepping on insects or bending a single blade of grass.

Bestiaries

In the European Middle Ages illustrated books called bestiaries described creatures thought to exist in the world. Unicorns and other fantastical animals appeared alongside elephants, donkeys, and bears. Older bestiaries show unicorns the size of goats, often blue in color. Later books depict white, horse-sized versions. Some features of unicorns never varied: the single horn and the fiercely solitary nature.

Maiden and Unicorn

This Italian painting from 1602 shows the unicorn as a small horse with a goat's beard. In European lore, unicorns were considered impossible to catch—unless you happened to be a young maiden sitting quietly under a tree.

Royal Coat of Arms

The unicorn joins the English lion on the United Kingdom's royal arms, symbol of the British monarch. On the Scottish version the unicorn also wears a crown.

TRACKING DOWN CLUES

Hey, look up there! On the ridge a graceful, horse-sized animal with a single straight horn gazes into the distance. Could it be a —

Nope. The animal turns, revealing a second horn.

Viewed from the side, antelope and similar four-legged, horned animals look a lot like the popular creature of myth. Such mistaken impressions may have helped to keep the unicorn legend alive. But a closer look confirms that most of these critters are missing an all-important feature — the unicorn's single horn.

So what was the animal described by Ctesias, the Greek doctor and writer who first sparked the legend? A likely suspect is the greater one-horned, or Indian, rhinoceros, known to science as *Rhinoceros unicornis*, or "one-horned nose-horn." Okay, the connection might seem like a stretch. Indian rhinos are huge — males reach twelve feet in length and can weigh over four thousand pounds, about four times bigger than a horse. A rhino's horn grows from the snout, not the forehead. But this shy and solitary creature would have been a common sight in northern India when Ctesias was collecting reports for his book. Indian rhinos are powerful, swift runners, too. And as a doctor, Ctesias would have been familiar with the long-held misbelief that rhino horn could cure illness.

So perhaps Ctesias combined accounts of the Indian rhinoceros with other, smaller animals, such as wild donkeys and Indian gazelles. Then he brightened up the results to produce the exotic, multicolored creature featured in his popular book.

Bingo, the unicorn.

Some scholars have suggested that the massive *Elasmotherium*, sometimes called the Siberian unicorn, influenced unicorn stories in eastern Asia. *Elasmotherium* was an enormous shaggy type of rhinoceros, more than eight feet tall at the shoulder, that roamed the plains of Eurasia until around thirty-nine thousand years ago. Rhinoceros horns, however, do not preserve well and paleontologists have not yet recovered the giant animal's horn from the fossil record. If and when they do, we will definitely hear about it!

Mystery of the Missing Horn

Elasmotherium, or the Siberian unicorn, grew a bony large dome on its skull that's not found on other rhinos. Did a magnificent horn sprout from that spot . . . or was the horn a stubby one as recent studies suggest? Paleo-artist Agustin Diaz shows both possibilities above.

Almost a Unicorn

The large antelopes called oryx have impressive horns. When seen from the side, these natives of the Middle East and Africa might easily be mistaken for unicorns.

The Sea Unicorn

The demand for unicorn horns skyrocketed during the Middle Ages, as royalty and other wealthy Europeans collected so-called "alicorns" to cure sickness and prevent poisoning.

In fact, most alicorns were actually the tusks of the narwhal, a medium-sized whale of Arctic waters. Male narwhals grow one long, straight tooth with spiraling ridges. The Inuit people have lived among narwhals for thousands of years, featuring them in hunting traditions and depending on them for food. Around 1590, Scandinavian sailors and merchants recognized the opportunity to sell these tusks to European markets.

Unicorn horns for sale! The tusks sold for several times their weight in gold, and the long, spiraled shape became the model for all depictions of unicorns. Narwhals are rarely seen farther south than Greenland, so clever sea hunters were able to guard the true identity of the "sea unicorn" for over two hundred years.

Worst Unicorn Ever

Back in 1663 fossils of a large animal emerged from a quarry near Magdeburg, Germany. Local scientist Otto von Guericke, best known for inventing the air pump, proclaimed the discovery to be . . . a UNICORN! With scant knowledge of anatomy or paleontology he combined parts of two Ice Age animals—the skull of a woolly rhinoceros and the shoulder blades and thigh bones of a woolly mammoth. As a finishing touch he added a narwhal tusk for the horn. Today the Magdeburg Unicorn is known as one of the worst fossil reconstructions of all time. Maybe Otto should have stuck to air pumps!

"There are wild elephants and plenty of unicorns, which . . . have a single large, black horn in the middle of the forehead. They spend their time by preference wallowing in mud and slime. They are very ugly brutes to look at."

—Italian explorer Marco Polo, c. 1300

The Dangerous Myth of Rhino Horn

After nearly going extinct in the mid-twentieth century, populations of Indian rhinoceros are slowly increasing due to conservation efforts. All the world's living species of rhinos face extinction because their horns are wrongly thought to cure fevers and other ailments. In fact, rhino horns consist of keratin, a fibrous protein found in nails, hair, and hooves that offers absolutely no medical benefit. You might as well chew on your own fingernails!

TO BE A UNICORN

At first glance unicorns seem pretty average compared to many other animals. Consider the giraffe with its impossibly long neck, or the scale-covered pangolin — those critters are truly bizarre! If we ignore mythical elements like disease-curing horns or rainbow farts, unicorns seem to fit easily into the group we call ungulates — large mammals with hooves, like horses. Its only unusual trait is that single bony spiral sticking out of its forehead.

Is a single horn really so far-fetched?

Let's consider how life-forms evolve. Many features of organisms alive today originated millions of years ago. This includes the basic organization and structure of bodies, called body plans.

Over five hundred million years ago, during what's called the Cambrian explosion, the body plans of major animal groups took shape. Some animals, like jellyfish and sea stars, acquired radial patterns that resemble daisies. A few, like sponges, developed irregular or asymmetrical forms. Many animals, however, evolved body plans that are bilaterally symmetric. Such bodies have heads, tails, and two halves that are mirror images. Insects, fishes, reptiles, birds, and mammals (including us) are bilaterally symmetrical. In the case of humans, this means we have two arms, two legs, and two eyes. Even our noses have right and left halves.

Yes, there are exceptions, such as the position of certain internal organs. But horned mammals like cows, sheep, bison, or gazelles all sport a pair of bony horns connected to the skull, with one horn on each side of the forehead. In contrast, a rhino's stubby horn consists of compressed, hairlike keratin fibers. It grows from the skin just above the animal's snout, rather than from the top of its head.

Not a great look for a sleek and stylish unicorn!

MAKE YOUR OWN UNICORN

One-horned animals might be the exception, but that doesn't keep people from trying to create unicorns of their own.

In the 1930s an American biologist at the University of Maine decided to test an idea. Professor Franklin Dove suspected that horns grow not from the skull, as previously thought, but from "horn buds" within an animal's skin. The bony cores of horns, he claimed, grow from these buds and later fuse to the skull bone below. If so, it might be possible to manipulate the buds into growing a single horn. This, according to Dove, explained the reports of "living unicorns" through the centuries.

For his experiment Dove transplanted the two horn buds of a newborn calf to the middle of its forehead, with one bud on top of the other. The result? The "Unibull"! Dr. Dove's hypothesis proved correct. The calf grew into a sturdy, one-horned, and thoroughly mischievous bull known for digging under fences and poking its cow friends. Dove's achievement inspired others to create unicorns from different farm animals. In 1985 a self-proclaimed wizard named Oberon Zell-Ravenheart applied a similar method to goats. One of his goats, called Lancelot, toured in the traveling circus company Ringling Bros. as a "living unicorn."

Animal rights activists soon put an end to these questionable practices, leaving generations of goats to enjoy their horns in peace.

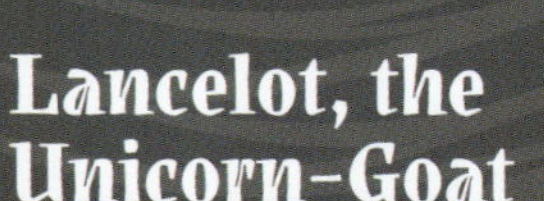

Lancelot, the Unicorn-Goat

Despite his fierce-looking headgear, Lancelot was known to be gentle and friendly.

"Do you know, I always thought Unicorns were fabulous monsters too? I never saw one alive before!"
"Well, now that we have seen each other," said the Unicorn, "if you'll believe in me, I'll believe in you. Is that a bargain?"

—Lewis Carroll, **Through the Looking-Glass, and What Alice Found There**, 1871

The famous Unicorn Tapestries portray the legend of a unicorn hunt.

Horse or goat, rhino or antelope. One thing is for sure —

WE LOVE UNICORNS!

For centuries Europeans believed the unicorn was a real animal inhabiting exotic, far-off lands. Today these beloved creatures live on in our imaginations, inviting escape into a realm of enchanted forests and dreams.

Now let's meet another type of legendary creature. It looks a bit more like you and me — but a whole lot bigger.

YETI

Shy Giant of the Himalayas

LET'S IMAGINE . . .

Three men are herding yaks to summer pasture, high above their village. It's late spring in the Himalayan Mountains, five hundred years ago. Rivers tumble past, swollen with meltwater from the springtime thaw. Waterfalls thread down sheer cliffs, catching rainbows in clouds of spray.

Up and up the herders climb, following rough stony paths through forests of bamboo and rhododendron and then higher still, past juniper scrub and over swaying rope bridges spanning deep rocky chasms. The shaggy beasts trudge steadily along, bells around their necks clanging in a noisy rhythm.

After long days of travel the men and their herd reach the wide-open alpine meadows. Great peaks loom over them. They'll spend all summer here while the yaks eat their fill of grasses and oak leaves.

Now the men search for a place to make camp.

"What is that?" One of them points at a black speck moving across a snowfield above them. They strain to see more clearly, but the figure drops over the ridge into the next valley and disappears from sight.

"Look," says another of the men. The others join him alongside a line of footprints, sharp-edged in the icy crust, that the creature left behind. A cold wind whistles down from the glaciers, biting their cheeks and bringing a smell that's unfamiliar and foul. What strange animal could they have seen that walks like a person, on two legs?

Through the grazing season the men search for more signs. Sometimes they hear a high-pitched scream that wakes them at night. They never see the two-legged figure again. Yet when summer ends, they return home with a story to tell — the wondrous tale of a not-quite-human creature that roams the high snowfields. The mysterious being that we know today as —

the yeti.

ROOF OF THE WORLD

Looking for a wild giant? If you're ready for some ice and snow, pack your bags for the world's highest mountain range — the Himalayas, often called the Roof of the World.

The Himalayas began forming around fifty-five million years ago, when the Indian subcontinent crashed into Asia, powered by the movements of Earth's outer shell, known as plate tectonics. The collision lifted a two-thousand-mile swath of rock to create the Tibetan Plateau, a vast region that contains nine out of the world's ten highest peaks. And it's not over yet — the Himalayas are still being pushed a couple of inches higher each year as the Indian plate grinds northward. The rugged landscapes of the region range from dense jungles to remote valleys and glacial peaks. A wealth of different animals inhabits these ecosystems, from snow leopards and marmots in alpine areas to bears, tigers, pandas, and others in mid-elevation forests and foothills.

Among the many different people of these mountain regions are the Sherpas, a group that began migrating from Tibet to Nepal in the fifteenth century. Sherpas make their living by farming, trading, and herding yaks. They are renowned for their climbing skills, expert navigation, and endurance on mountaineering expeditions. Sherpa traditions encompass Buddhist practices and animism — the belief that spirits inhabit rocks, caves, trees, and other objects in nature. They hold the high peaks in great reverence and refer to what Western society calls Mount Everest as Chomolungma, meaning "Mother of the World."

Oh yes! We have many kinds of wild animals in these forests. There are bears, and musk deer, and yeti, and pandas, and leopards, and civets, and monkeys, and many, many more.

—an Arun villager of Nepal, quoted in **The Arun** by Edward W. Cronin, 1979

Yeti on a Mountaintop

Artist Tashi Lama created this Tibetan-style painting, or **thangka**. It shows snowy peaks, including Everest and Makalu, surrounded by monasteries, villages, herds of yaks and sheep, and lush, forested hillsides. Do you see the bear, the red fox, and the mountain goat? What about the wild boar, musk deer, frog, or pheasant? And don't forget the yeti, sitting atop a mountain to one side!

LEGENDS AND LORE

They're wild. They're hairy. And they smell really bad!

Giants show up in folklore traditions across the globe. In legends these powerful, humanlike beings are often solitary and wild. Most importantly, they are huge — anywhere from a few feet taller than an average person to the size of mountains. Some mythical giants are considered to be a type of "cryptid" — animals believed by some to be real but whose existence has yet to be proved.

The yeti ranks among the most famous of the cryptids. The name "yeti" — derived from the Sherpa word *yeh-the*, meaning "animal of rocky places" — represents one of several names and identities for this creature among mountain-dwelling people of Nepal, Bhutan, China, and Tibet. Many traditions tell of an enormous, not-quite-human animal with blackish-brown hair and a taste for eating mosses, frogs, and furry little alpine animals called pikas. In some stories the beast howled, whistled, or shrieked. In other tales it flew through the air or had backward feet and a bad smell. It could be a friendly creature that brought food to hermits in their caves . . . or a dangerous kidnapper of children. In general the yeti was best left alone.

Early European visitors to the Himalayas reported sightings of a "wild man" covered with long dark hair. Word spread as foreign explorers set their sights on climbing Chomolungma, which was named Mount Everest by European surveyors in 1865. In 1921 a British expedition reported seeing footprints that, according to their local guide, belonged to a *metoh-kangmi*, or "man-bear snow-man." A journalist mistranslated the phrase as "filthy snowman." He modified the wording to "abominable snowman" — and the yeti frenzy began.

Abominable! Shocking! Mountaineers encouraged the hype in order to raise funds for their adventures. The Nepalese government joined the action by issuing special yeti hunting licenses. In 1951 another British expedition produced photographs of large, humanlike footprints. More monster hunters joined in, from rich Texas oilmen to famed mountaineers. The yeti captured the public imagination with movies, books, and comics depicting a fluffy white snowman. Yet despite costly expeditions over the decades, evidence remained thin. Interest began to fade, but the question remained: What was leaving tracks in the snow?

The whole story seemed like such a joyous creation that I sent it to two or three newspapers.

—Henry Newman, journalist who coined the term "abominable snowman" in 1921

This drawing from the 1950s shows a group of hikers spotting a yeti, or abominable snowman, in Nepal.

INTERNATIONAL GIANTS

Why do so many cultures feature humanoid giants in their mythologies? Some legends might have been triggered by discoveries of fossils like those left by the jumbo-sized animals of the ice ages known as "megafauna," such as mammoths, saber-toothed cats, and giant ground sloths. Others may be linked by "cultural memory" to long-ago times when people shared the landscape with those now-extinct animals. Stories arose, to be told and retold . . . and giants grew bigger with each retelling.

CYCLOPS

The legendary one-eyed Cyclops of Greek mythology is sometimes linked to the fossilized bones of dwarf elephants found on Mediterranean islands (*top*). When those bones are assembled to mirror the posture of humans, the skeleton looks like a fifteen-foot-tall humanoid giant. The large hole where the elephant's trunk would have attached could easily be mistaken for the hole of a single giant eye. This statue (*middle left*) from around 150 BCE shows Polyphemus, a man-eating Cyclops featured in Homer's epic tale, the *Odyssey*.

MAPINGUARI

Like the Cyclops, this fearsome giant of Brazil was said to have only one eye. The Mapinguari sported a second mouth on its belly. As depicted here (*middle right*) by artist Ray Troll, the furry creature is sometimes linked to giant ground sloths that evolved in South America and overlapped with humans for thousands of years.

SASQUATCH

The Sts'ailes people of British Columbia, Canada, tell of the *sasq'ets*, a shape-shifting creature that inhabits and protects the wilderness (*bottom*). Sasquatch exists in the traditions of Indigenous people of the Pacific Northwest. Some non-Native fans of Sasquatch — or "bigfoot," as it is sometimes called — suggest that these giants represent a branch of the yeti family.

Not Quite Human

Yetis and similar creatures were thought to inhabit a realm of existence somewhere between human and nonhuman. Sometimes, as depicted on this Bhutanese postage stamp, they grew to enormous size.

TRACKING DOWN CLUES

Calling all yetis! It's time to measure those big furry feet!

For a century the search for the yeti focused on footprints. Western travelers photographed tracks of various sizes, suggesting a population of adults and their young. A large, humanlike animal was out in the snow, walking on two feet. What was it?

One possibility was the world's largest known ape: *Gigantopithecus*. Based on fossilized teeth found in 1935, followed by discoveries of more teeth and a few jawbones, this plant-munching giant was estimated to have reached ten feet in height. It lived in southern China from roughly two million to three hundred thousand years ago — unless, as some people speculated, its descendants had survived to modern times.

Hold on! An animal of that size would need enormous amounts of plants to eat, far more than are available in the high Himalayas. And analysis of proteins from *Gigantopithecus* teeth reveal that its closest relatives are orangutans — knuckle-walking apes of tropical forests on the islands of Borneo and Sumatra in Southeast Asia. In other words, those remains were no match for the yeti.

So how about some kind of long-lost human? Several species of humans have shared the landscape of central Asia over time. Could the yeti be a group of now-extinct humans? If so, where are their artifacts, fossils, or other signs of life?

One man, Daniel Taylor, devoted three decades to solving the mystery. Taylor grew up in the Himalayas. As an adult he trekked into remote valleys and over snowy passes. He gathered stories from Sherpas and other Indigenous peoples. Gradually two legends emerged. One told of small, tree-dwelling creatures. The other featured a frightening giant.

Next, Taylor reexamined photographs of yeti prints and found signs of claw marks. Humans and other primates do not have claws — but bears do! Taylor knew that bear tracks look like those of humans when the bears' hind feet step into the imprint made by their front feet. This is a common pattern for how bears walk. Add the blurring effect of melting and refreezing snow, and you've got yourself . . . a humanoid giant. Taylor studied the tracks of tranquilized bears in a zoo and determined that footprints attributed to the yeti were actually made by Himalayan black bears, a species that is most active at night. When young the animal is arboreal, spending much of its time in trees. When it grows bigger, it moves to the ground. This behavior, changing through a single bear's lifetime, can explain the stories of two separate creatures.

Daniel Taylor went on to lead the conservation of vast parklands in the Himalayas. Today those valleys, mountainsides, and forests provide habitat for bears, pandas, leopards, and other wildlife . . . and maybe even a yeti.

So-Called Scalp

In 1953 New Zealand explorer Sir Edmund Hillary and Sherpa mountaineer Tenzing Norgay achieved the first summiting of Mount Everest. Hillary returned to the Himalayas in 1960, intrigued with finding the yeti. A monastery allowed him to borrow a precious relic—the alleged scalp of a yeti. Upon study it was found to be constructed from the hide of a serow, a goatlike antelope common to the region.

Famous Footprints

In 1951 British explorer Eric Shipton claimed to have taken photographs of yeti footprints in Nepal. The prints, clearly outlined in the snow, measured thirteen inches long. Later, however, some of Shipton's companions revealed that he enjoyed making jokes. Was the famous explorer pulling a prank?

Bears and Leopards, Oh My!

The Himalayan black bear (**top**) can be recognized by its white, V-shaped chest marking and bell-shaped ears. It's one of the largest tree-dwelling mammals but takes to the ground full-time as an adult. Snow leopards (**bottom**) inhabit alpine meadows and rocky areas. Their eerie calls during mating season may help to explain reports of the yeti's howls.

Yes, You Are an Ape

Humans are primates, a group of mammals with large brains and grasping hands that have fingernails rather than claws. Within primates we belong to the subgroup known as hominids, or great apes. The greatest—or at least the biggest—of all known apes is **Gigantopithecus**, a giant that once inhabited the warm, wet forests of southern China and Vietnam. This painting by John Sibbick shows **Gigantopithecus** sharing the landscape with one of our human ancestors, **Homo erectus**, around 1.8 million years ago.

TO BE A YETI

Don't close the book on the yeti just yet.

Within the last 150 years or so, several so-called "mythical" animals have been confirmed as members of the zoological world. They include the giant panda (1869), mountain gorilla (1902), and Komodo dragon (1912). Coelacanths, a type of fish thought to have gone extinct around sixty-six million years ago, showed up alive and swimming in 1938. Could yetis be next on the list?

Let's consider this from a scientific perspective. Science is a step-by-step process for making sense out of natural phenomena. A researcher makes an observation and forms an idea, or hypothesis. Then they collect evidence and use that data to test the hypothesis. If their conclusions support the hypothesis . . . hooray! The researcher gets busy writing down and sharing the results. If not, they reject the hypothesis or rethink the procedure.

To confirm the idea of a new species (including a shaggy alpine giant!), scientists need proof of an actual body. This could include DNA, fossils, or other physical remains. For living creatures they can also consider evidence of a "Minimum Viable Population" — the smallest number of animals required to meet, mate, and produce offspring within a geographic area. In the case of gorillas or other large mammals, that's at least three hundred individuals. After a century of searching, however, not a single yeti has been found across the vast Himalayan regions. No verified body parts have been found either. The math does not look great.

Maybe that's okay. After all, what would happen if someone captured a yeti? Would it be dragged off to a zoo? Forced to pose for photographs? Perhaps these wild beasts are better off staying safely in the mythical realm.

Here's the advice I'd give a yeti: Don't let them find you! Don't let them cut your hair, silence your howls, or slap shoes on your oversized feet. Be a night prowler, a snow dweller, a champion of the world's loftiest heights. Be rare and rough and yet to be discovered. Find your way to far-off horizons . . .

and leave nothing but footprints behind.

DNA DOES NOT MELT

Footprints in the snow tend to melt and change shape. But not DNA!

DNA is the molecule in all living things that carries genetic information — the instructions needed for growth and functioning of a living organism. Working like crime scene detectives, scientists can identify organisms by analyzing DNA extracted from the cells of body parts. DNA from the cells of saliva, mucus, or poop works too.

In 2013 a film company contacted scientist Dr. Charlotte Lindqvist about analyzing the DNA of "yeti" specimens. Her team analyzed nine samples, including fur, bone, teeth, and hair that had been found in the Himalayas. Eight of the samples confirmed the link to bears. The ninth was from a dog. The film company was disappointed with the results — but Dr. Lindqvist was thrilled. Using the new data, she was able to build a genetic profile of wild bears that can help protect the species into the future.

Another DNA expert, Dr. Todd Disotell, works with bigfoot enthusiasts across North America. In addition to producing documentaries and joining expeditions, he analyzes samples in his lab. So far, results have yielded evidence of bears, coyotes, deer, people, and other known animals — but no mysterious giants. Dr. Disotell, however, keeps an open mind. Bigfoot quests are fun . . . and who knows what you might find?

A Talent for High Places

Yetis might be the stuff of stories, but some other two-legged animals survive quite well in the high Himalayas. Many people of Tibetan origin live at altitudes above sixteen thousand feet, a height at which most people quickly grow sick. How do the people of Tibet do it?

Turns out that Tibetans carry a unique variant of a gene that increases the oxygen-carrying capacity of their blood. Amazingly, the "superathlete" gene can be traced to an extinct human population: the Denisovans, who ranged across Asia from around three hundred thousand to thirty thousand years ago. Researchers first discovered Denisovan fossils inside a Siberian cave in 2010. A jawbone fragment showed up later on the Tibetan Plateau. But the highest proportion of Denisovan genes appears in certain populations to the east of Tibet, in the Philippines.

Were Denisovans passing through the Himalayas on their way to warmer climes? A recent fossil discovery—a complete jawbone, found in Taiwan—seems to confirm this hypothesis. We'll never know the details, but it's reasonable to say that Denisovans met and mated with modern humans in the area sometime around forty-six thousand years ago. Then they moved on, leaving behind a talent for endurance among today's residents of the Roof of the World.

Like other natives of the Himalayas, this child in the Dolpo region of Nepal (**right**) may have inherited an adaption for high-altitude survival from a long-ago human ancestor.

Science illustrator Maayan Harel created this image of a Denisovan girl using information from samples of ancient DNA.

I don't ever say it does not exist, because science can't say that. But if it does exist, I have tools to help identify it.

—Dr. Todd Disotell, geneticist, evolutionary biologist, and cryptid-TV star

Many of us are fascinated by giants, the jumbo-sized humanoids that are bigger and stronger versions of ourselves. Maybe it's because we all start out small, as children surrounded by gigantic grown-ups (hairy, big-footed, sometimes grumpy!). But the scariest creatures aren't always the biggest. Sometimes they are slippery, sneaky, and dripping wet. It's time to leave the high mountains of Asia and journey to the shores of the Land Down Under — Australia.

A very scary creature awaits.

BUNYIP

Beware of the Water!

LET'S IMAGINE . . .

A family gathers around the fire on a lakeshore in South Australia some five hundred years ago. Smoke rises from the oven mounds, fragrant with the smell of roasting bulrush roots, emu, and fish. The sounds of daytime are fading — the laugh of the kookaburra, the honk and splash of ducks. From the dusk comes a chorus of frogs and the distant call of a black swan.

As the first stars twinkle overhead, three children slip from the darkness to join the safety of the circle. They are muddy and scratched, and their voices shake. They've seen something by the water, they exclaim — a creature half hidden in the gloom, with glowing eyes and a groaning voice. The children ran away fast, but it followed them, they're sure of it! The children stretch their arms to show the size of the creature —

Then they stop. Their eyes go wide, catching the glimmer of firelight.

And a low, slow call echoes from the reedbeds.

Boom-boom. Boom-boom.

Everyone falls silent.

Finally Grandfather begins to speak. "We know the story," he says, "of young ones who went too close to the riverbank after the sun went down. The Mulgewongk grabbed one and took him down into a cave under the river."

The children wait, open-mouthed.

"So the people got one of the old men," continues Grandfather. "They rubbed him with fat so he could breathe underwater and be safe. They gave him feathers, too."

The grown-ups nod. Grandfather raises his hands. "When the man came to the cave, he started waving the feathers and singing. So he put the Mulgewongk to sleep. Then he got the little boy and took him up to his mother and father. And that boy never, ever went alone to the river again. That's one story the Elders told."

The children huddle closer. Without a word, they make a promise to each other — they will always stay away from the water's edge at night, when the Mulgewongk is awake.

The old fellow. The bad spirit of water.

The creature that many people today call —

the bunyip.

Adapted from a traditional Ngarrindjeri story, "The Mulgewongk's Cave," as told by the late Uncle Henry Rankine. Special thanks to Mark Koolmatrie, Ngarrindjeri elder, and Philip Clarke of the South Australian Museum for their help and review.

A DRY PLACE TO LIVE

This scene adapts a story of the Ngarrindjeri people, who have lived along the Lower Murray River and South Australia coastline for many thousands of years. Like all Aboriginal Australians, the Ngarrindjeri connect deeply to the natural world — in this case, the vast ecosystem of Australia's largest river, the Murray, known as the Millewa or Tongala in Aboriginal languages of the area.

Much of Australia, however, is dominated by dry inland plains known as the Outback. Based on the latest archaeological evidence, the first Aboriginal people began arriving to the island continent around sixty-five thousand years ago. As they spread out, they developed ingenious strategies to survive. Some people learned to recognize desert plants and animals that signal the presence of water — small birds, for example, like zebra finches or peep-wrens. They shared myths and songs that identified the locations of hidden springs and pools known as billabongs. They found water in the trunks of desert oak trees and as dew droplets on leaves. Some accounts even tell of digging up frogs from underground during the summer heat. A quick squeeze of a water-holding frog into a thirsty mouth — ah, refreshing! The frog is then carefully reburied so it can survive.

When the British First Fleet arrived in 1788, Aboriginal Australia included over two hundred language groups and clans spread over varied landscapes. Colonization had devasting impacts on the Aboriginal way of life, including loss of ancestral homelands and separation of children from parents. Yet the people endure. Today they represent one of the world's oldest continuous cultures, with traditions finely tuned to the rhythms of the land — including the many dangers posed by water bodies, small and large.

After all, who knows what might lurk just under the surface?

The Outback

Australia is the world's driest inhabited continent. A natural water hole, like this one at Watarrka National Park at the center of the country, provides a refuge for many plants and animals.

The laughing kookaburra, a native bird of Australia.

LEGENDS AND LORE

Is it a carnivorous kangaroo? A sharp-clawed bird? A snaggle-toothed reptile? YES! All these and more — it's a bunyip.

Like the water it inhabits, the bunyip takes on many shapes. Through the years some reports have described the bunyip as a four-legged mammal with long, shaggy hair and fangs. Others mention an enormous starfish or a unique combo of emu, crocodile, and wallaby. A bunyip might have feathers or scales. It might swim like a frog, slither like a snake, or grow thirteen feet tall and walk upright on land.

So . . . what is it? The modern-day word "bunyip" probably originated as *banib* in a Wemba Wemba language of southeastern Australia. The *banib* is one of many names for water spirits — like the Mulgewongk of Ngarrindjeri tradition — that gave rise to the bunyip myth. Most share several common features. The bunyip is secretive and amphibious, moving between water and land. It is not a Dreamtime Ancestor from the time of creation long ago, but rather a spirit-being that shares the landscape with people. And the bunyip is dangerous, especially for children.

When Europeans came to southern Australia, they accepted the bunyip as one of many animals that were unfamiliar to them. After all, what could be weirder than the platypus, an egg-laying mammal with a duck's bill? Or those gangly kangaroos bounding across the grasslands? Newspapers in the nineteenth century reported many bunyip sightings. Some people dismissed these as misplaced seals, sea otters, or crocodiles. Others remained convinced that bunyips were out there, waiting to be found.

Gradually, as European settlement expanded, the bunyip's reputation became less threatening. It even made its way into books for children. In *Dot and the Kangaroo*, published in 1899, the bunyip is a scary, gully-dwelling demon. Fast forward to 1973, with the publication of the picture book *The Bunyip of Berkeley's Creek*. The hero of that tale is a harmless fellow searching for his identity across the Australian countryside.

Along the Lower Murray River today, reports of the Mulgewongk have become less frequent as boat traffic claims the waterways. But who knows? One moonless night, while you sit by the campfire, a bunyip might climb a muddy bank, sneak up behind you . . . and give you a good Australian scare.

Bright-Eyed and Bellowing

Descriptions of bunyips often include two particular features: glowing red eyes and a deep, booming roar that can be heard for miles around. Yikes!

This bunyip, created for a children's book in 1900, combines a dog's head with enormous tusks and webbed claws.

All Sorts of Scary

No matter what forms they take, bunyips are usually associated with ponds, lakes, and rivers. **The Bunyip of Berkeley's Creek**, a picture book written by Jenny Wagner and illustrated by Ron Brooks, features a charming character who travels with a handy mirror and comb.

The Bunyip

You keep quiet now, little fella,
You want big-big Bunyip get you?
You look out, no good this place.
You see that waterhole over there?
He Gooboora, Silent Pool.
Suppose-it you go close up one time
Big fella woor, he wait there,
Big fella Bunyip sit down there,
In Silent Pool many bones down there.
He come up when it is dark,
He belong the big dark, that one.
Don't go away from camp fire, you,
Better you curl up in the gunya.
Go to sleep now, little fella,
Tonight he hungry, hear him roar,
He frighten us, the terrible woor,
He the secret thing, he Fear,
He something we don't know.
Go to sleep now, little fella.
Curl up with the yella dingo.

—by Oodgeroo of the Tribe Noonuccal

Other Creepy Crawlers

Around the world, tales of evil spirits warn children to avoid dangerous waters. Rusalka (**above**), the water nymphs of Slavic mythology, are ghosts of young women who lure men to watery graves. Their loose greenish hair must stay wet for them to survive, and they carry combs made of fish bones. In Japan the kappa or "river boy" (**right**) is a turtle-monkey-frog chimera with straggly green hair. A kappa carries water in a bowl-shaped depression atop its head. Despite its eerie nature, it will always politely return a bow—at which point the water from its bowl spills and the kappa loses strength. Remember that the next time you encounter this mischievous imp!

TRACKING DOWN CLUES

Bunyips take many different shapes and sizes. Where do we even start?

Possibilities abound. Australia has been an isolated landmass for over thirty million years, setting the stage for the evolution of unique animals and plants. The continent is home to two-thirds of the world's marsupials — mammals whose babies are born tiny and hang out in pouches or skin pockets. And don't forget monotremes, the mammals that lay eggs. These two groups include wonderful animals such as wallabies, numbats, quill-covered echidnas . . . not to mention oh-so-adorable koalas. The list goes on!

And that's not all. During the ice ages — the Pleistocene Epoch, from 2.6 million to 12,000 years ago — many types of animals grew to enormous sizes. We know them from the fossils they left behind in many places across the world, including Australia. Time for some quick arithmetic! Australia has been inhabited by humans for some sixty-five thousand years. That means that some of the continent's remarkable megafauna overlapped with Indigenous peoples for tens of thousands of years.

To be clear — these animals were ginormous. The sight of a monstrous creature emerging from the local water hole would have made a lasting impression — one that would be handed down in stories, artwork, dances, and songs. These encounters may be more than "myths" in the sense of something invented; they might well be memories of real experiences, passed down from ancient ancestors. Imagine running into a gigantic diprotodon, for example, on your way to fill a water jug. These massive wombat-shaped creatures — the largest marsupials of all time — lived across Australia until around forty thousand years ago and reached six thousand pounds in weight. (Compare that to their distant cousins, the impossibly cute wombats of today, weighing about eighty pounds at the most.)

The many wonders of Australia's natural world, present and past, suggest that there may be multiple inspirations for this water spirit. Scary, elusive, and especially dangerous to young ones — beware of the bunyip!

Mega-Lizards Rule the Land

If you could time-travel back fifty thousand years in Australia, you'd find giant kangaroos and enormous flightless "thunderbirds" nibbling plants alongside enormous diprotodons. Sounds like a peaceful scene . . . but who's this? Meet the mega-lizard known as **Megalania**. Like a scaled-up version of the Komodo dragon, this largest of all terrestrial lizards reached over sixteen feet long. An ambush predator and scavenger, Megalania held the top spot in ancient Australian food chains. And did I mention the possibility of venom?

On second thought, that trip through time might not be such a great idea.

Most Terrifying Award

Not scared by **Megalania**? Indigenous people also shared water sources with now-extinct predators like the leopard-sized marsupial lion **Thylacoleo (right)** and the slightly smaller Tasmanian tiger **Thylacinus (left)**. Could one of these fearsome animals have informed early tales of the bunyip?

Current Suspects

The duck-billed platypus (**below**) feeds and burrows in swampy river edges and streams. Like the bunyip, it is a solitary critter that's active from dusk to dawn. The Australasian bittern (**right**)—sometimes called the "bunyip bird"—is a secretive nocturnal animal that inhabits wetlands of southern Australia. It's best known for its distinctive call. **Boom-boom, boom-boom!**

TO BE A BUNYIP

Dripping and dangerous, the bunyip rises from Australia's ancient past like a hungry swamp creature. Its physical form might be hard to pin down — is it a giant lizard? a half-human gremlin? — but tales of bunyips and other water spirits have enlivened Australian storytelling for countless generations.

Why is the bunyip so enduring? Australia is already famous for life-threatening animals. They've got stinging stonefish and paralysis ticks, lethal bees and venomous snakes, and, in the northern states, some of the meanest saltwater crocodiles around. With all these to choose from, why tell stories of a deadly water spirit that refuses to emerge from the shadows?

Perhaps the bunyip simply reflects the hazards of inland waters. For Aboriginal people and European newcomers alike, one thing never changes: the desire to keep children safe. This water spirit may take many different shapes, but they all serve as warnings to be careful around rivers and lakes.

From ancient times to today, the bunyip comes alive in the call of a bird, the splash of a platypus, and the jaws of every fierce predator sneaking to the water's edge for a drink.

The bank is slippery. The current is strong.

The dangers of the water's edge are very real, indeed.

The Case of the One-Eyed Bunyip

Among European settlers, bunyip excitement reached a peak in the 1840s, when a strange one-eyed skull turned up along the Hawkesbury River in southeastern Australia. The discovery soon attracted a crowd at the Colonial Museum of Sydney. At last, declared enthusiasts, we know what a bunyip really looks like! The idea spread like wildfire. People began reporting more and more strange sounds and dark shapes near the water at night. The bunyip was close by—people were certain of it.

The buzz ended, however, when a naturalist named William Sharp Macleay correctly identified the finding. Be more careful in your scientific process, he warned. This was no bunyip—merely the head of a deformed baby horse. Today you can find Macleay's own specimen, the so-called Bunyip Cyclops, at the University of Sydney's Chau Chak Wing Museum.

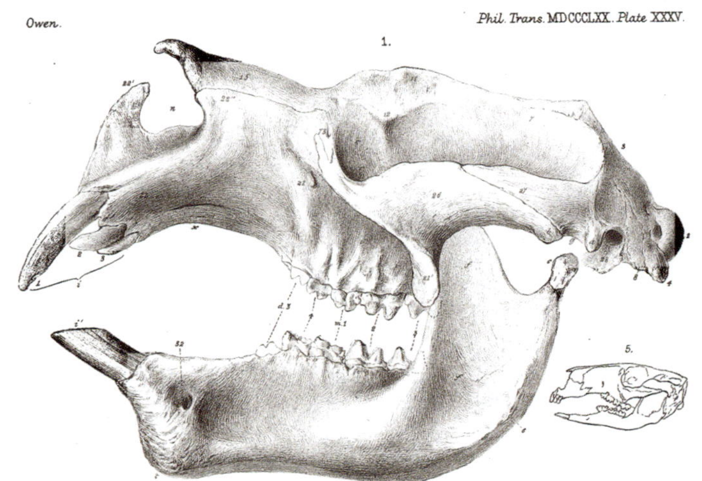

Skull of **Diprotodon optatum** in a British illustration from 1870.

Dreamtime Stories

For Aboriginal people, Dreamtime stories speak of events from the time of creation. During the Dreamtime, supernatural ancestors—often in the form of animals—traveled across Australia and gave form to its landscape. Over many thousands of years and across multiple groups, the Dreamtime stories passed from one generation to the next. They connect listeners to the natural world and offer guidance for living a good life.

This painting by the Tjapukai people, who live in Australia's northeastern state of Queensland, celebrates some of the continent's iconic animals.

The giant marsupial known as diprotodon, illustrated here by wildlife artist Peter Trusler, overlapped with early Indigenous people in Australia before going extinct around twenty-five thousand years ago. The massive plant-munching animal may have contributed to bunyip legends and others.

Water might be dangerous, but we can't live without it. Throughout history people have made their homes next to rivers, lakes, and oceans. From those watery realms come stories of mythical beings of many kinds.

In the next pages we'll travel over the waves to another continent that's south of the equator. There we'll meet a water creature that's lovelier than the bunyip, perhaps . . . but no less treacherous.

MERMAID
A Dangerous Beauty

LET'S IMAGINE . . .

Three men paddle up the Niger River delta, a thousand years ago. Their dugout canoe, laden with salted fish, sits low in the rain-swelled stream. For weeks they've been traveling to the market town on the shores of a lake. But which way to steer? They've taken this route before, but the year's heavy floods have erased any familiar landmarks. Instead of a steady current to guide them, the water swirls and eddies in all directions.

They are lost.

In the bow, the youngest man peers into the flooded forest. He's been crouching here all night, on the lookout. His head spins with hunger and heat and the buzzing of insects. His eyelids drift closed.

Splash! The man jerks awake, expecting a crocodile. Instead, a womanlike form rises from the blanket of fog. The creature holds a child in her arms.

A flood of homesickness sweeps over the man. How he misses his village, his parents, his wife who holds their newborn baby just like this! The forest noises melt into a song — *join us, join us* — and he leans over the side of the boat.

"Brother!" the others cry out. They pull him back — but as the woman slips under the water, the man catches a glimpse of a tail. A fish's tail!

"That way! She guides us!" he calls, and points to the ripples where the creature disappeared. Together the men turn the canoe hard to one side, into a tangle of mangrove trees. They duck down low, make a final push — and the forest opens to the wide expanse of a lake, lit by the rosy glow of dawn.

They cheer, and the young man looks back one last time. There's no sign of the mysterious being, and he wonders . . . who was she? Was she showing him the way . . . or tempting him to danger? Long after the fish are sold, after the journey home to coastal breezes and open skies, he tells of a womanly figure rising from the mist. Half fish, half human. The story changes through the years, blending with other tales of danger and beauty, of spirits that dwell in the magical realm between water and air.

The realm of the mermaid.

MAMI WATA

Lakes and rivers, wetlands and streams — the many waterways of Africa have given rise to a rich variety of water spirits. In stories passed from generation to generation, many spirits embodied snakes or crocodiles. Some were half fish and half human. For thousands of years, traditional tales explained the mysteries of creation and the natural world.

Over time many water spirits merged into one — the powerful Mami Wata, or Mother Water. Often linked to West Africa, Mami Wata is also celebrated in central and southern parts of the continent, as well as in coastal locations of the Americas, like Cuba and Brazil. Her identity overlaps with other water goddesses, such as Yemaya, a deity from the Yoruba religion. Mami Wata expresses the fluid nature of water and its various identities. She can heal the sick and bring good luck, but she has a sharp temper and will drown those who disobey her wishes. She is often portrayed as a mermaid, a snake charmer, or both. Her mermaid form may link to the carved figureheads of European sailing ships that once traveled the African coast. Sometimes she takes on features of Hindu deities brought by merchants from India.

With Europeans came the devastation of the transatlantic slave trade. African people were torn from their homes and crowded onto ships bound for the Americas. Many died along the way. Those who survived faced the atrocities of forced labor. Along with these resilient people came folklore of tricksters, shape-shifters, and spirits of nature. Stories, artwork, and beliefs endured, helping enslaved people maintain identity and strength. Today Mami Wata and other water spirits of Africa come alive in new expressions on both sides of the Atlantic Ocean.

Flowing Hair, Slithering Snakes

Mami Wata is often shown with flowing hair, a half-human and half-fish body, and snakes around her neck. This poster, inspired by a famous German snake charmer in the 1880s, became a popular image in Africa and beyond.

The Slave Ship Brooks

In this painting, Haitian artist Frantz Zephirin depicts a deity of the sea swimming alongside a slave ship, ready to guide lost souls back to their homeland. British opponents of slavery prepared the original image of the **Brooks** in 1788 to communicate the horrors of the slave trade to the public.

LEGENDS AND LORE

Mermaids are everywhere!

For thousands of years these alluring creatures have been swimming into stories and myths all around the world. Accounts of mermaids vary from place to place, but many share details in common. Why do mermaids in Europe, Africa, and the Americas all carry mirrors and combs? And why are they so attractive and dangerous at the same time?

Let's start with the basics. A mermaid is a mythical sea-dwelling being with the upper body of a woman and the tail of a fish. An early depiction dates back to 1000 BCE with Atargatis, a powerful Assyrian goddess who dove into a lake and became a fish from the waist down. Ancient Greeks loved their merfolk too. The Nereids, for example, were beautiful sea nymphs who lived in harmony with ocean creatures and protected sailors.

So far, so good. But in many traditions mermaid lore took a darker and more ominous tone. Was this because people both love and fear the vast, unexplored oceans? Or do we simply enjoy scary stories the most? No one knows, but Greek mythology provides some threads to follow. In addition to Nereids ancient Greeks told of sirens — dangerous bird-women who lured sailors to shipwreck with their songs. Siren stories mixed with those of mermaids, resulting in tales of gorgeous enchantresses who sprawled on rocks, combing their hair and admiring themselves in mirrors, waiting to drag sailors into the inky black depths.

This portrayal spread with the expansion of naval trade. Mermaid figureheads sometimes adorned a ship's bow in hopes of calming the seas and finding safe harbor. Yet in sailor folklore, mermaids represented both good fortune and disaster. Would they rescue you from a storm or pull you to a watery grave? Mermaids were slippery creatures who moved between water and air — lovely and serene above the surface, mysterious and dangerous below.

Despite their dubious reputation mermaids continued to delight. In medieval Europe they were considered real ocean animals alongside dolphins or fish. Another idea of the time held that all land organisms had a counterpart in the sea. Everyone knew about seahorses, sea wolves, and sea snakes . . . so why not half-human sea maidens too?

Nowadays we celebrate mermaids as beings who inhabit unfamiliar realms of the sea. Next time you're near the water, imagine yourself as one of them. Flip your tail. Let the tide untangle your seaweed-green hair. Dream of swimming with the whales, past sea caves and octopus havens. Be a deep-sea mermaid, sleeping on a bed of pearls.

Point your toes together — and dive.

Aye, tough mermaids are, the lot of them.

—Blackbeard, English pirate who sailed the West Indies and eastern coast of North America (c. 1716)

Mermaid Off the Starboard Bow!

In 1900 John William Waterhouse painted this image of a lonesome mermaid with long hair and pearly trinkets. Mermaids are part of the merfolk, a term that includes all half-human mythical beings of the sea. The English word for mermaid comes from "mere" (Old English for "sea") and "maid" (a girl or young woman).

A WORLD OF WATER SPIRITS

Water spirits pop their heads up in all wet places of the world, from warm tropical seas to icy fjords, freshwater springs, and muddy riverbeds. Whether protective and kind or frighteningly fierce, each fills a distinctive role in the traditions of their people and place.

Lasirèn

Ningyo

Lasirèn The Haitian spirit Lasirèn rules over wealth. She brings love and success to her worshippers but lures others to the ocean's depths. Artist Myrland Constant used beads and sequins on fabric to create this **drapo**, or flag, showing the mermaid with her mirror and comb. The flag, created in the years between 2000 and 2010, measures 33 by 43 inches in size.

Ningyo Japanese stories depict the ningyo as a fish with a human head. They can be omens of dark times ahead. Prepare for war if you find one of their bodies washed ashore!

Etruscan Sea-Girl

Etruscan Sea-Girl Ancient Etruscans of central Italy represented female spirits with bodies of birds or fish. This bronze statuette dates from the 6th century BCE.

Mermaid of Mexico This skeleton mermaid from the coastal region of Oaxaca celebrates Día de los Muertos, the Day of the Dead, by playing her yellow violin.

Caesg, Maid of the Wave

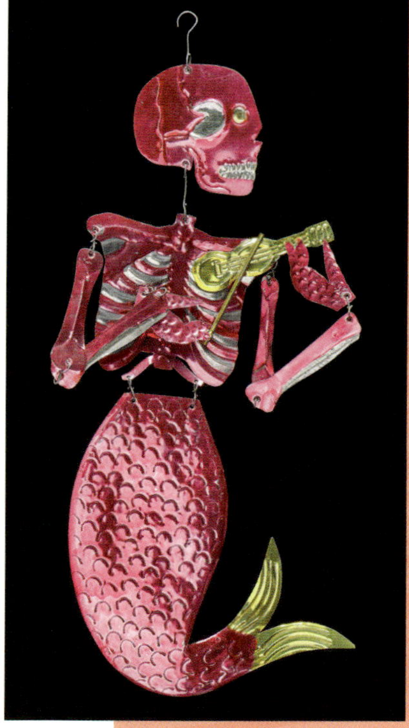

Mermaid of Mexico

Ceasg, Maid of the Wave Mermaids of the Scottish Hebrides islands, which are off the west coast of the mainland, are said to grant wishes or curses, depending on their moods. In the Outer Hebrides, the dreaded Blue Men are said to lay siege to passing ships; the only way to pass unharmed is to win a rhyming match against them.

Yawkyawk Long before Europeans arrived, the Australian Aboriginal spirit known as Yawkyawk held the form of a woman with a fish's tail. A Yawkyawk starts out in a tadpole-like form and develops a fish tail as it grows up. If you see a string of seaweed floating by, it may be a Yawkyawk's hair!

Sedna The Inuit people of northern Canada tell the story of Sedna, guardian spirit and mother of all sea mammals. In some tales Sedna was tossed overboard by her own father but survived to create the whales, seals, and walruses on which the Inuit depend for food.

Yawkyawk

Sedna

Atargatis According to legend, Atargatis accidently killed her sweetheart, a handsome young shepherd. In her grief she dove into a lake in hopes of becoming a fish, but the transformation only partially worked, and she became a mermaid instead. This sculpture from the Nabataeans, an ancient Arab people, dates from around 100 CE.

What About Mermen?

Even before Atargatis jumped into a lake, the fish-god Ea was bringing wisdom to the people of Mesopotamia (now south-central Iraq). This Babylonian stone seal from around 600 BCE shows Ea's characteristic beard, crown, and fish tail. Aspects of Ea, also known as Oannes, reappear in Greek mythology with Triton, messenger and son of the sea god, Poseidon.

TRACKING DOWN CLUES

Wow, mermaids are popular! What could have shaped their stories?

Many experts point to manatees and dugongs — the large, roly-poly aquatic mammals that make up a group of animals known as sirenians. These gentle "sea cows" resemble walruses, but without tusks. They have short front flippers, flat tails, and round heads and eyes. Like all mammals that live in water, they must come up to the surface to breathe.

Dugongs may have sparked the early mermaid legends of Ea and Atargatis. They swim in warm coastal salt waters from eastern Africa to Australia, and ancient seafarers would have spotted them while traveling from Babylonia and Assyria through the Persian Gulf. In the Pacific island nation of Palau, prehistoric cave drawings of dugongs are linked to tales of young women transforming into sea creatures. The dugong's name stems from the Malay word *duyung*, meaning "lady of the sea."

African manatees inhabit a wide range of West African waters, from offshore islands to upstream rainforest rivers. When African people reached the Americas, they would have encountered the West Indian manatee — a similar, slightly larger species. Farther inland in Brazil and neighboring countries, they might have seen the river-dwelling Amazonian manatee.

Okay, but what about colder areas? Dolphins are a possible influence. They range through temperate and tropical waters across the globe. Seals live in even colder regions including the Arctic and Antarctic. But let's face it — none of these marine mammals look like a lovely, svelte mermaid.

Perhaps we need to consider the life of a sailor. On watch through another long night, bleary-eyed and bored, he spies an animal's head among the moonlit waves. There's something out there . . . or is it someone? He squints. The creature stares back. It looks almost human yet most certainly at home in the sea.

Could it be a mermaid?

Manatee Moms

Sirenians use their flippers to grip objects—they even have tiny fingernails—and females hold their babies much like human mothers cradle a child. Although some manatees grow to be thirteen feet long and weigh 1,300 pounds, they are graceful swimmers and can reach speeds of twenty miles per hour.

Manatees and dugongs inhabit calm, tropical waters, especially coastal lagoons, rivers, and shorelines. Believe it or not, sirenians share a common ancestor with an unlikely distant cousin: the elephant! These peaceful, plant-eating aquatic animals are in danger of extinction primarily due to the impacts of motorboats, habitat loss, and pollution.

INSIDE A SCAM

By the 1800s, belief in mermaids as real animals had largely disappeared. That did not stop showman P. T. Barnum from exhibiting the "FeeJee Mermaid" in his circus. Barnum advertised with a picture of long-haired, fish-tailed beauties basking in the waves. Thousands of people bought tickets — only to find a shriveled, horrifying specimen on display instead.

Barnum's exhibit ignited a craze. Mummified merfolk had long held a place in the Shinto shrines and temples of Japan. Now dozens of museums and sideshows in Europe and America wanted one too. Hoaxers sped up production, often by sewing a monkey's head and torso to the tail of a fish. Hideous? Yes. Did people love them? Also yes!

Some "mermaids" even went beyond bizarre animal mash-ups. When London's famous Horniman Museum took a close look at their "Japanese Monkey-fish" mermaid, they saw that the head was not a monkey's at all. So they examined the insides using X-rays and CT scans. Turns out their specimen was constructed from a fish's tail and fins sewed to (drumroll, please . . .) a frame of wood and wire, coated with clay and papier-mâché. Add a fish's jaw and pointy teeth — plus chicken's claws for the hands — and you're ready to start selling tickets.

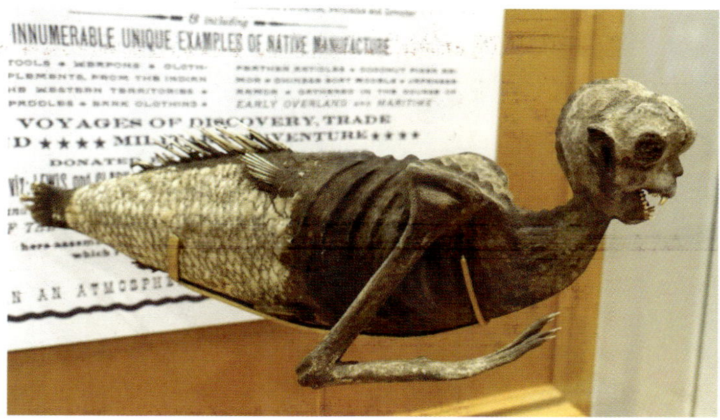

FeeJee Mermaid shown in P. T. Barnum's Museum in 1842.

Definitely Not a Mermaid

Yes, some fish can hang out on land! Mudskippers trap a bubble of air in their gills before leaving the water, then absorb oxygen through their skin. They use leglike front fins to wiggle-hop across the mud and can even climb roots and low branches. But these bug-eyed little creatures are definitely NOT mermaids.

TO BE A MERMAID

First let's define the merfolk as half human, half fish. We'll assume they need to breathe underwater like fish (after all, they dwell in those fabulous deep-sea castles) and also breathe air when they visit the surface.

No big deal, right?

Well . . . maybe. One problem is that humans, like all mammals, pull air into their lungs. Most fish use gills — organs on the sides of their heads — to extract oxygen from water. These distinct methods for breathing date back millions of years.

Another challenge is getting food. Fish are adapted for underwater hunting. Many fish suck prey into their mouths by opening their jaws to create a vacuum. Some fast predators, like sharks, have mouths bristling with sharp teeth. Humans lack any of these adaptations. Our teeth evolved for grinding rather than snagging and tearing up our meals — and we certainly lack vacuum-cleaner mouths.

Merfolk could, of course, survive by munching on ocean plants. But here's another problem: Any humanlike creature would have trouble staying warm underwater. Because of its greater density, water conducts heat away from the body twenty-five times faster than air. Marine mammals like whales have evolved insulating layers of blubber and thick, rubbery skin. The outer layer of a dolphin's skin, for example, is fifteen to twenty times thicker than a land mammal's skin. Manatees have slightly less blubber, but this isn't a problem because they stick to warmer waters. They're also protected by tough, wrinkled skin, like that of an elephant.

In comparison, the thin skin of a human would soon become water-logged and break down. If you or I spent that much time in a mermaid's lair, the water pressure would reduce our blood circulation and make breathing impossible. We'd quickly become chilled. Our internal organs would stop working, and . . . well, you get the idea.

So, could a mermaid exist? To survive as an aquatic humanoid, you'd need thick, leathery skin and a solid layer of blubber. You'd want to be bigger to maintain body warmth. You'd need special eyes to see underwater too.

In other words, you would end up looking a lot like . . . a manatee.

Becoming Mermaids

If you open your eyes underwater, everything looks blurry. The children of the Moken "sea nomad" tribe of Thailand, however, have developed the ability to adjust their eye lenses and pupils to focus when they are submerged. Seals and dolphins have a similar adaptation. And it turns out that other kids can do this too, with practice. Adults lose the skill as they age, which is why the Moken tribe leaves diving to the youngsters.

Mermaid Training

Every year, aspiring mermaids travel to Florida's historic Weeki Wachee Springs State Park in hopes of becoming a performer in the park's famous mermaid show. They must pass grueling auditions and undertake months of training—turns out it's not easy to be graceful while doing backflips in a fish tail! Weeki Wachee Springs offers a Junior Mermaid camp too, for ages seven to fourteen. At Weeki Wachee and elsewhere, many mermaid performers consider themselves to be spokespeople for conservation of the world's ocean.

Diving for Treasure

Japanese divers known as Ama—"women of the sea"—specialize in free-diving deep into bone-chilling cold water to gather abalone, shellfish, or pearl-bearing oysters. The tradition dates back some two thousand years. Then, as now, the divers exhale with a special "sea whistle" to regulate their breathing between dives.

The Little Mermaid

One of the most famous Western stories of merfolk is "The Little Mermaid" by Hans Christian Andersen. Published in 1837, it tells of a mermaid who falls in love with a land-dwelling prince. Andersen's original tale doesn't work out so well for the poor mermaid, but recent retellings usually offer a happier ending. Danish sculptor Edvard Eriksen created a bronze statue for the Copenhagen harbor inspired by the story. It is said to be the most photographed statue in the world.

> **She had never danced so elegantly before. Her tender feet felt as if cut with sharp knives, but she cared not for it; a sharper pang had pierced through her heart.**
>
> —Hans Christian Andersen, **The Little Mermaid and Other Tales**, 1837

Scary and beautiful, dangerous and enticing — merfolk move between worlds, from fishlike to human, from watery depths to familiar shorelines. With them comes the enchantment of magical stories . . . and plenty of trouble.

And what happens when sea creatures grow very, very big? It's time to leave the safety of shore and venture farther out to sea. There we'll meet a monstrous ocean dweller that rarely comes to the surface at all. But when it does — watch out!

KRAKEN

Tentacles from the Deep

LET'S IMAGINE . . .

Three storms on the open sea.

It's late summer in the year 1400. A crew of Wokou pirates struggles through a typhoon howling up the Sea of Japan. They crest a wave, and the ship jerks to a stop. The deck tips. The mast creaks. The helmsman screams as a massive creature wraps its tentacles around the ship's stern. For a moment the sailor stares into its green glowing eyes — the eyes of the dreaded sea monster known as Akkorokamui. Then the ship shudders and begins to move again.

The monster is gone.

A century earlier, Polynesian explorers follow the pathways of stars across the South Pacific. A cyclone closes in, obscuring the skies. The travelers watch the ocean swells and the rising winds. They track the flight of an albatross, high overhead. Sailing southward, ever southward, they spy a long, low island on the horizon. Years later some will call this place New Zealand — but the first explorers give it the name Aotearoa, Land of the Long White Cloud. And there, as they come ashore, they find a massive multilimbed creature stranded on the wave-tossed beach.

What could it be?

Across the globe and another hundred years back into the past, a family travels from Norway to a new home in Iceland. For weeks they battle hurricane winds, constant downpours, and rolling seas. They huddle among cargo and farm animals, shivering and drenched. At last the storm clears. The ship's navigator sighs in relief — now he can read the starry map that's painted in the heavens.

Two sisters shake off their blankets and run to the rail. Salt spray stings their eyes. "Look!" cries the older girl. She sees something between the swells, like huge fingers beckoning to her. "Gudrid, look!"

The navigator steps closer. "What do you see?"

"A serpent! There!" She points. The navigator's face turns pale. He pulls the children aside and surveys the thrashing waters. He's heard warnings of a gigantic beast that can drag an entire ship to the bottom of the ocean. Largest of all sea creatures, they say, with a craving for human flesh.

And the child has seen it, right off the starboard bow.

Sea monster of the deep . . . the kraken.

A BAD CASE OF THALASSOPHOBIA

Here's a question: Would you climb aboard a wooden boat, wave goodbye to family and friends, and sail across the uncharted ocean in hopes of finding new land? By the way, you've got no compass. No radar, radio, or GPS — and no guarantee of a return trip home.

Many people would answer with a definite NO WAY! In fact, the prospect of such a venture might trigger a bad case of "thalassophobia," meaning the intense fear of deep bodies of water. Yet throughout human history, seafaring cultures have launched voyages that succeeded beyond all odds, expanding human settlement to new continents and islands across the globe.

No group of navigators is more renowned than the Polynesians. Sailing in double-hulled canoes and outrigger boats, these intrepid adventurers explored the vast expanse of the Pacific Ocean for thousands of years. They developed sophisticated navigation techniques by observing stars, wind and wave patterns, and birds and other marine life. Polynesians reached as far east as Easter Island (also known as Rapa Nui) and Hawaii. They even sailed from Indonesia to Madagascar off the African coast — a daunting five-thousand-mile voyage across the Indian Ocean.

The Vikings used some of these techniques too. From the ninth to the eleventh centuries, these Scandinavian seafaring warriors invaded and colonized wide areas of Europe. Their famous longships were light, flexible vessels that carried raiders into battle. The *knarr*, a wider craft with an open central space for cargo, transported settlers and traders.

No matter their origin or destination, all seafarers faced the hazards of ocean storms — not to mention the dangers of deep-sea monsters lurking in the watery depths.

Stormy with a Chance of Monsters

Reports of kraken sightings are often linked to the powerful, spiraling storms that form over oceans. Those storms take different names depending on location. **Typhoons** develop in the Northwest Pacific while **hurricanes** wreak havoc over the North Atlantic, central North Pacific, and eastern North Pacific. **Cyclones** develop in the Southern Hemisphere over the South Pacific and Indian Ocean.

Kupe and the Octopus

According to legend, the first Polynesians to New Zealand were led by Kupe, a brave navigator and warrior chief who was chasing a giant octopus that was stealing fishing bait. The chase led Kupe and his companions across the sea. After a 2,500-mile journey, they made landfall in what is now called New Zealand and established its founding people, the Māori. This scene of a later event, painted by Augustus Earl in 1827, shows Māori warriors preparing to set off in swift-moving **waka**, traditional warcraft canoes.

LEGENDS AND LORE

The kraken is slithery and strange, island-sized and alien. Rising from the murky ocean abyss, it terrorizes sailors, fishermen, and seafarers across the globe.

Let's face it — you couldn't ask for a better sea monster.

Few mythical creatures evoke more fear than the mighty kraken, a massive beast with sucker-lined tentacles, huge glowing eyes, and an insatiable appetite. One of many such legends from around the world, the kraken stems from the folklore of medieval Scandinavia, where people lived close to and on the sea. The name derives from the Old Norse verb *at kraka*, meaning to "drag downward."

Early mentions of the kraken date to the year 1200, when an ancient text called the *Physiologus* was translated into the Icelandic language. Among many other animals both real and fantastical, the text described a gargantuan, bottom-dwelling whale known as hafgufa, meaning "sea mist." This terrifying creature reportedly swam the Greenland Sea, where it occasionally burst through to the surface, sinking ships within its deadly, swirling whirlpool.

Over the centuries hafgufa morphed into the multilimbed kraken: a fearsome monster that could pluck a sailor from the deck with its tentacles and blacken the waters with its foul ink. (Krakens used the whirlpool trick, too!) In 1755 a Danish bishop described a squid-like beast that resembled a floating island — but when a sailor stepped on its back for refuge, the kraken would sink and drown them in the depths.

Krakens were blamed for the disappearance of fishing boats or voyaging ships. They were impossible to kill. Even the bravest sailors feared the kraken's enormous size — bigger, it was believed, than the largest of the Norse ships.

Kraken stories spread in the nineteenth century with the expansion of the whaling industry. In the classic book *Moby-Dick*, published in 1851, writer Herman Melville described the so-called "devil-fish" as a huge, pulpy monster with "innumerable long arms radiating from its centre, and curling and twisting like a nest of anacondas." Another famous author, Victor Hugo, detailed the horrors of a swimmer being devoured alive by the malignant, repulsive beast.

The sea monster made its way into recent times, too. "Release the Kraken!" is a famous quote from *Clash of the Titans*, a fantasy movie released in 1981 and reprised in 2010. Krakens appear in the swashbuckler film *Pirates of the Caribbean*, in books like *Artemis Fowl*, and as an amphibious monster in the role-playing game Dungeons & Dragons.

These dramatic tales are designed to thrill. But if we scale the monster to a smaller size and tone down its ship-sinking, sailor-munching habits . . . we may discover one of the most fascinating real-life animals to ever swim the seas.

"What was it, Sir?" said Flask. "The great live squid, which, they say, few whale-ships ever beheld, and returned to their ports to tell of it."

—Herman Melville, **Moby Dick**, 1851

Pull Out the Hatchets!

In the 1870 science fiction novel **Twenty Thousand Leagues under the Sea**, author Jules Verne described a gargantuan squid attacking the crew of a submarine. Tentacles flail, hatchets chop, ink flows! The book was a smash hit, launching the kraken into popular culture.

Le poulpe brandissait la victime comme une plume. (Page 396.)

MONSTER SOUP

This might be a good time to have "that talk." You know, the one about . . . MONSTERS.

Monsters are more than just oversized animals. They might be otherworldly and alien. They might have sharp fangs or two hideous heads. They might even be eerily beautiful, like the half-human mermaid. The truth is that monsters are thrilling and horrifying, all at the same time. They shine a light on what we do not understand, and our imaginations fill in the rest.

Maritime lore overflows with vicious monsters. The Leviathan of ancient Hebrew legend was an evil serpent, so immense that the sea frothed and boiled when it emerged at the surface. In Greek mythology the six-headed monster called Scylla haunted a rocky coastal passage and preyed upon passing sailors. Maps from sixteenth-century Europe show visions of oversized lobsters, sharp-fanged fish, and "sea monks" that combined features of fish, squid, and Christian monks.

Amid the monster soup of ocean legends swims the kraken, most monstrous of all.

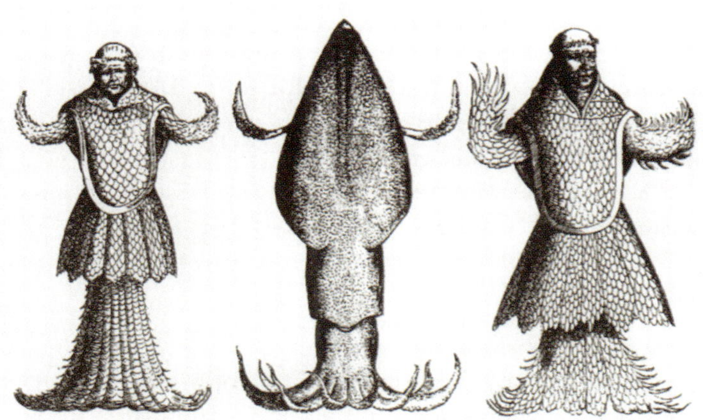

TRACKING DOWN CLUES

Okay, we got this one.

As you may have guessed, a likely clue to the kraken's origin is the giant squid. These enormous invertebrates rarely emerge from their ocean homes at depths of one thousand to three thousand feet. Their elusive nature ignited a debate that raged for many years. On one side were seafarers with eyewitness accounts. Whalers, for example, noticed circular scars on the skin of sperm whales, left by the squids' sharp-edged suckers. They also found what looked like enormous parrot beaks inside the whales' stomachs. Some kind of sharp-beaked, tentacled creature lived far under the waves — they were sure of it.

Before the discoveries of modern times, scientists dismissed these accounts. Nothing could possibly survive in the gloomy ocean depths, they said. The temperature was too cold, the pressure too intense. If an animal doesn't dwell near the surface, they reasoned, it can't exist at all.

Nevertheless, more reports came in. In 1848 the captain of a British ship reported on a huge, many-limbed creature near the southern tip of Africa. The crew of a French steamship spotted a giant squid in the middle of the Atlantic and captured a partial specimen. In 1857 a Danish zoologist gave the animal an official scientific name: *Architeuthis dux*, meaning "most important squid leader."

Still, experts dug in their well-polished heels. Nonsense! How could we not already know about such an enormous animal? Other findings, like squid carcasses found on shore, did little to settle the argument. Decaying on a beach, a squid's body quickly turns into a slimy mush that's impossible to preserve or transport. In other words, the evidence simply falls apart. Also, like you might expect from a rotting sea creature . . . it STINKS!

Finally, in 1873, two fishermen in Newfoundland, Canada, spotted a large animal floating in the water below the cliffs. Curious, they steered their boat closer and poked the quivering mass — which shot out at them at lightning speed. One man grabbed an axe, chopped at the squid, and returned to shore with definite proof — two nineteen-foot-long tentacles.

At last the giant squid was confirmed as a part of the zoological world, distinct from the legendary kraken but no less mysterious.

QUEST FOR THE GIANT SQUID

The quest to understand the giant squid has become one of oceanography's greatest challenges. Yet until recently no one had managed to even catch a glimpse of a living specimen.

Dr. Edie Widder, a marine biologist and explorer, came up with a hypothesis: Could the noisy engines and bright lights of underwater submersibles, she wondered, be scaring the giants away? Using her experience with bioluminescence — the light that some organisms generate inside their bodies — she devised a silent optical lure called the electronic jellyfish, or e-jelly. The lure imitates the bioluminescent display emitted by a deep-sea jellyfish when under attack by a predator. The display is intended to attract even bigger predators — like giant squid — and allow the jellyfish to escape. Dr. Widder and her team combined the lure with a camera system, called the Medusa, that uses a wavelength of red light invisible to the squid.

Success! Using the new equipment, explorers caught live footage of a giant squid as it followed the e-jelly, then struck the lure at lightning-quick speed. This thrilling observation revealed that giant squid are active and efficient hunters rather than ambush predators as previously thought. Maybe they are a bit like krakens after all.

"We've only mapped 5 percent of the ocean bottom. There are great discoveries yet to be made down there, fantastic creatures representing millions of years of evolution and possibly bioactive compounds that could benefit us in ways that we can't even imagine."

—Dr. Edie Widder, oceanographer and inventor

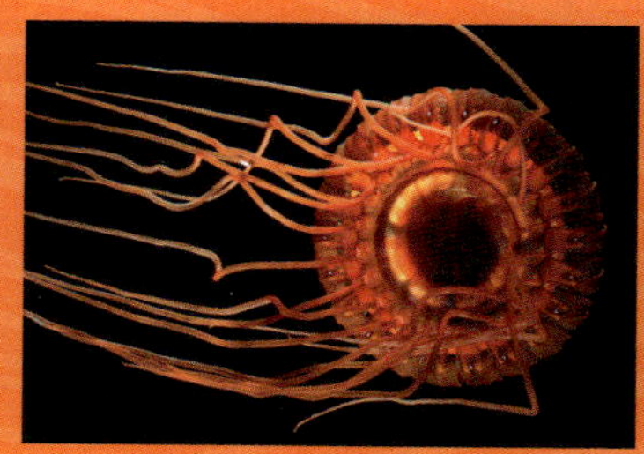

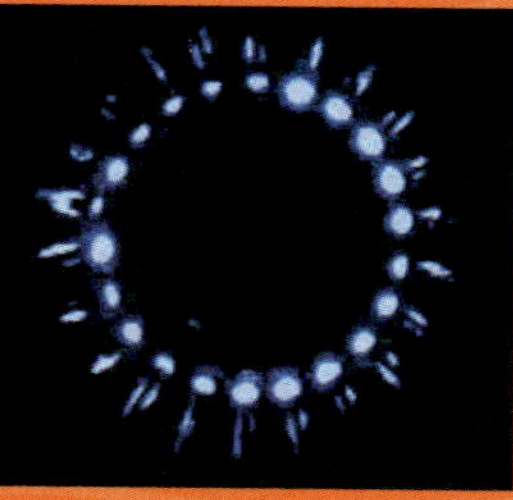

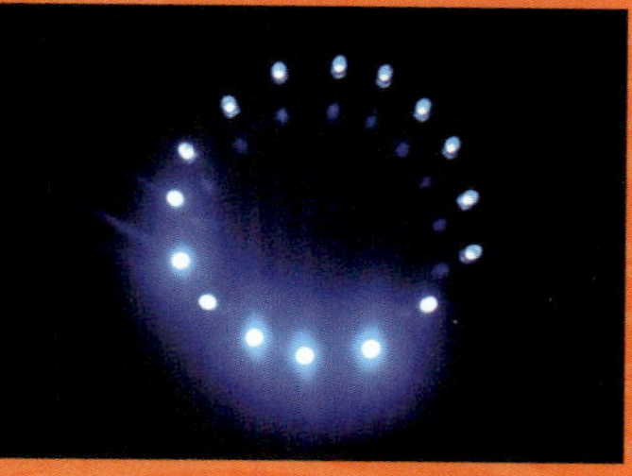

The jellyfish **Atolla wyvillei** and its bioluminescent "alarm display" (**left and center**). The e-jelly at work, mimicking its living counterpart (**right**). Using the lure, the Medusa camera system recorded footage of two live giant squids, first in 2012 near Japan's mainland and again in 2019 in the Gulf of Mexico.

A diver photographed this giant squid in the Sea of Japan. The mottled colors indicate that the animal's skin is peeling.

Nineteen Feet of Tentacles

In 1939 American painter N. C. Wyeth illustrated the scene of two fishermen fighting off a giant squid near the cliffs of Conception Bay, Newfoundland.

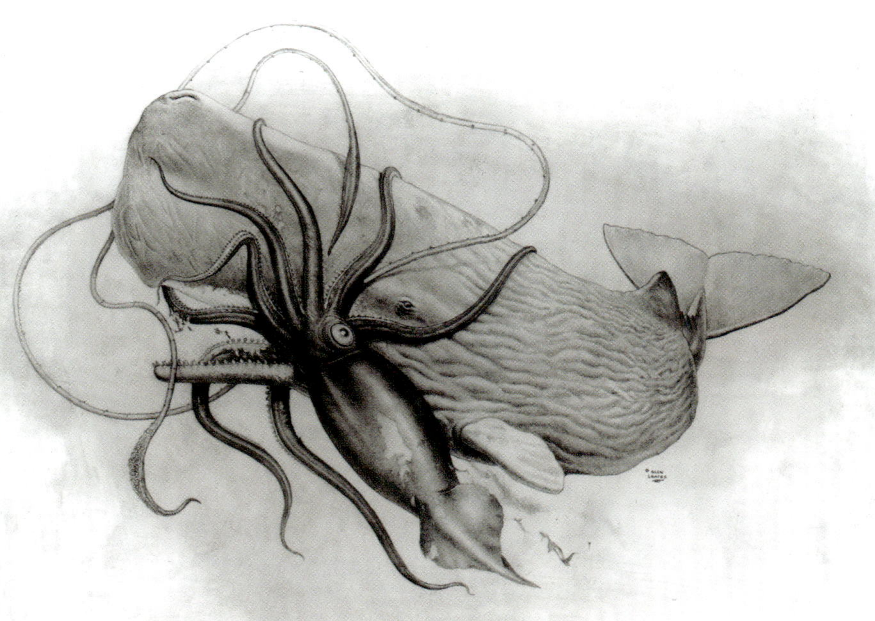

Whale Versus Squid

Giant squid sometimes leave circular scars on the skin of sperm whales—evidence of battles between the two mighty giants, far below the waves. Squid have eight arms, like their octopus cousins, plus two longer feeding tentacles.

TO BE A KRAKEN

Could a squid grow to monstrous proportions and become a kraken?

Animals adapt to their environments in many ways, including physical size. In general, body sizes within a population will change through time depending on what is advantageous for survival. Let's say that a genetic mutation occurs, producing a distinctly larger individual. For whatever reason — an ability to more effectively avoid predators, for example, or find food or a mate — that individual produces more offspring. The trait for larger size can then be passed down. Over a long stretch of time this process of natural selection sometimes results in an entirely new species — such as a ferocious, multilegged monster roaming the vast ocean.

Impossible? No. Likely? Well, the jury's out.

In the meantime we can learn some lessons from the mythical kraken.

To be truly legendary . . . be yourself! Give your admirers a few hints — a wave of a tentacle, a glimpse of your gorgeous, humongous, glimmering eyes. Not too much! A quick appearance will keep your fans properly terrified and busy talking about you during long trips at sea. Then go for it! Build on your reputation as elusive, powerful, and just plain large. If your popularity takes a dip, feed the fire with a few surprise appearances. Hug the occasional fishing boat in your magnificent arms. Ride to the surface on a stormy day and frighten a boatload of pirates out of their wits. Let the tales grow. Finally you can claim your place as master of the murky and mysterious deep (but watch out for whales!).

Be hungry. Be different. Be difficult to find. And if they get ahold of you — raise a terrible stink.

HOW TO MAKE AN OCEAN ALIEN

Let's start with a squishy, forty-five-foot-long, torpedo-shaped body. Next add eight arms and two tentacles lined with hundreds of jagged-toothed, prey-grabbing suction cups. How about a sharp, parrotlike beak for ripping apart flesh, plus gigantic eyes as big as your head? Finally let's equip our alien with blue blood, three hearts, nine brains, and a built-in jet propulsion system for swimming forward or in reverse at top speed.

Put it all together, and you've got a giant squid! Your creature may look bizarre to us landlubbers, but these animals are supremely adapted to life in deep oceans. Their soft, squishy bodies enable them to withstand tremendous water pressure. Their eyes — the biggest of all known animals — allow them to detect small amounts of light in the deep. Giant squid inhabit all parts of the world's ocean, except for polar and tropical regions. A common location for giant squid sightings is the North Atlantic — birthplace of the kraken legend.

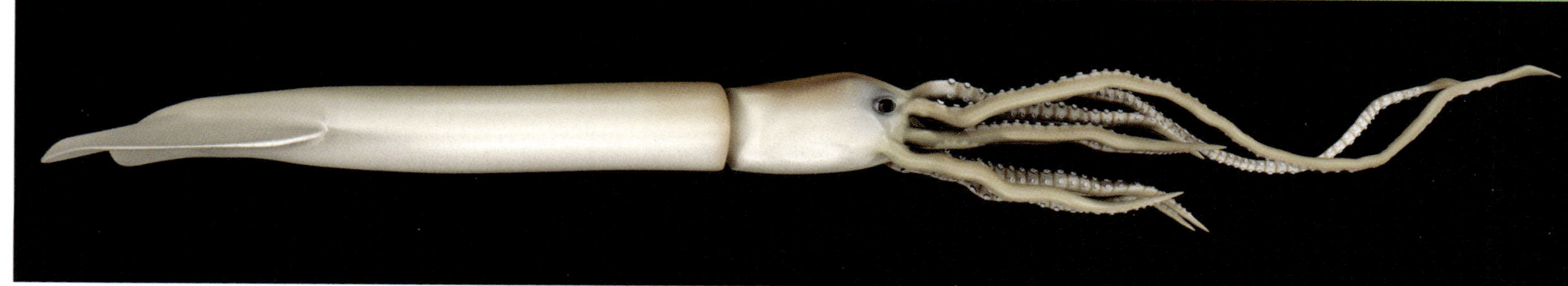

Sea Monsters Overhead!

In 1883—a decade after those Newfoundland fishermen chopped two tentacles off a mysterious animal floating near the shore—the International Fisheries Exhibition in London suspended a bug-eyed cephalopod model over the heads of well-dressed Victorian ladies and gents. Giant squid were all the rage!

Sea monsters like the kraken connect us to the vast ocean — the place where all life began. Yet our knowledge of deep-sea environments amounts to no more than the tip of a tentacle. There's a whole world under there, waiting to be explored.

For now let's leave the watery realms behind. We'll travel from Iceland to Ireland and discover another of life's great wonders — the miraculous power of flight. It's time to go airborne!

FAIRIES
Beguiling Spirits

LET'S IMAGINE . . .

A harvest celebration is underway in Ireland, four hundred years ago. Amid the bonfires and dancing, a girl named Fiadh slips away and walks toward the darkening woods, leaving the cottages and neatly plowed fields behind.

A barn owl swoops past on its evening hunt. Behind a spreading oak, Fiadh finds a familiar path. Trees close overhead. Shadows deepen, but her feet know every twist and bump. She clambers down a slope, and the forest opens onto a pond lit by the lingering glow of dusk.

The girl stands at the water's edge. She can't explain what pulls her to this wild place, in the moments between daylight and dark. Perhaps it's the rustle of wind in the reeds. The water lilies, with their soft white petals folding inward for the night. Or the swans that float so quietly, followed by their fluffy gray young.

She's waiting for something. What is it?

A full moon peeks above the trees, and its light sparkles on the pond. There's a sudden movement — a dart and swoop of something airborne and tiny. Dragonflies! Their wings shimmer. Their bodies gleam ruby and green and gold. One of them comes closer and closer. Fiadh stumbles back. The insect circles her head. The drone of wings roars in her ears as the little creature hovers, pivots, flies straight — and hits her square in the forehead. There's no pain, nothing more than a tap. No more than a kiss.

Fiadh hurries home with mud on her boots and twigs caught in the hem of her skirt. She seeks out her sisters, eager to share her story. But when the moment comes to tell them, something holds her back.

The dragonfly's kiss will be her secret, always.

Fiadh grows up to be a healer, renowned for crafting potions from mushrooms and herbs and night-blooming lilies. The villagers keep their distance, coming to her only at times of illness or childbirth. She consorts with the Good People, they whisper to each other. *Na Daoine Maithe* — the Fair Folk, the Sídhe. The charming, unpredictable spirits that have come to be called . . .

the fairies.

THE EMERALD ISLE

At the far western edge of Europe lies the lush green island country of Ireland. Some twelve thousand years ago icy glaciers scraped the land bare, leaving behind a rocky landscape of hills and valleys, meandering waterways, remote lakes, and damp, peaty bogs. Over the centuries this rugged and isolated setting has given rise to a rich folklore rooted in the mysteries and beauties of nature.

Irish storytelling dates back to the Celts, a collection of tribes from central Europe who reached Ireland around 700 BCE. They thrived there for two thousand years, resisting waves of invaders. Even when southern Britain fell under Roman rule, the Irish Celts — along with the fierce Picts of northern Scotland — remained unconquered.

Divided into small kingdoms, the Irish Celts kept busy fighting among themselves. Warriors held special rank, as did the blacksmiths who crafted weapons. Both women and men served as druids — a Celtic name for healers and priests — and as bards, the poet-singers who composed and recited heroic tales of battles, romance, and mythical lands.

Today the cloudy skies and bright rainbows of Ireland continue to inspire stories of magical spirits. Watch for them when the veils between worlds grow thin, such as the Celtic New Year at the end of harvest season, known as Samhain, or the festival of Beltane at the start of summer.

Welcome to Fairyland

Bernard Sleigh, an English artist, sketched a landscape of mythical stories to entertain his children. The **Anciente Mappe of Fairyland** was published in 1917.

LEGENDS AND LORE

Fairies are creatures of dewdrops, of ancient trees and hidden caves, of starry skies and fragrant blossoms. Their realm lies both inside and beyond our world. But beware! Once you enter that magical place, you may never return.

We often think of fairies as small winged sprites, like *Peter Pan*'s Tinker Bell, yet these enchanting creatures have taken many forms over time. Fairies have long held prominent roles in the folklore of western Europe. The name itself stems from the Latin term *fatum*, meaning "fate," and the Old French words *faerie* or *fae*.

Starting over a century ago, fairy experts (yes, that's a thing) began to distinguish between two major types of fairies. Trooping fairies lived in groups, enjoying parties, dancing, and mischief. While lovely and occasionally kind to people, they were known to steal babies and leave behind "changelings" — strange, nonhuman creatures that were reported to have big heads, beards, and enormous appetites. They also kidnapped children or adults, whisking them off to fairyland for a hundred years or more.

Solitary fairies included the famous leprechauns — wizened little men who worked as shoemakers and buried their pots of gold, playing tricks on anyone who tried to steal a single coin. Banshees were straggle-haired female spirits who wailed when someone was about to die. Some fairies shared human homes and even helped with chores. If the enchanted beings felt unappreciated, however, they transformed into more troublesome forms.

Over time the fairies of western Europe came to be known as nature spirits that dwelt in gardens and forests. Early stories described them as people-sized, but fairies of many traditions shrank in stature over the centuries. They reveled in moonlight and adored music and games. They inhabited trees, rocks, fields, or pathways — parts of the landscape that must be protected to avoid their wrath. Fairies hoarded treasure, it was said, that would turn into clumps of dirt in human hands. Only a few types could fly, usually through magic or by riding on birds.

In the nineteenth century, as the natural world came to be better understood, fairies took on a more friendly, whimsical role in artwork and stories. Writers and artists began depicting them as tiny creatures with wings.

And with that, fairies took flight!

Ancient Roots

Fairy lore arises from many different cultures and traditions. In older legends, fairies often embodied dangerous and mysterious powers of the natural world. Only in recent times have they come to be known as miniature-sized creatures with wings. In the British Isles, fairy legends are often associated with ancient Celtic mythologies, including those of the Picts, shown here, a tribal confederation that inhabited Scotland from around 300 to 900 CE.

Fairy Versus Elf

Elves are often considered to be a type of fairy. Folklore of elves, gnomes, pixies, and sprites originated in northern Europe. Elves are said to dwell in forests rather than gardens, are generally of a larger size, and usually lack wings. If all else fails, look for the pointy ears!

Brownies and Boggarts

According to British folklore, a helpful brownie could change into a thieving boggart that broke dishes or left sharp thorns in a bed. Regular gifts of food, such as porridge and cream, kept a brownie feeling happy and appreciated.

Riders of the Sídhe

Irish poet William Butler Yeats wrote of the Tuatha Dé Danaan, an ancient tribe with supernatural powers. When defeated by the invading Gaels—the people who came to be known as the Irish—they retreated to an underground realm and became known as the Sídhe, or people of the mounds. This 1911 painting by John Duncan depicts the Sídhe riding out on the May festival of Beltane.

Shifters and Tricksters

From many lands come stories of secretive, humanlike beings with powers linked to nature. Some are tricksters, cunning and eager to pull pranks. Others are shape-shifters that can change physical form. And some are both!

In Persian mythology a peri is a fairylike being thought to be descended from fallen angels.

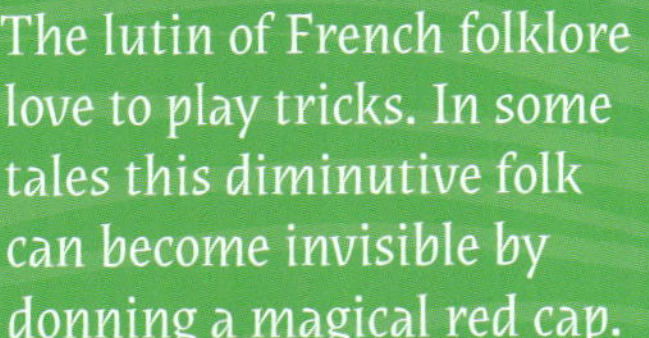

The lutin of French folklore love to play tricks. In some tales this diminutive folk can become invisible by donning a magical red cap.

Kitsune of Japan are fox spirits—sometimes called fairy foxes—that can shapeshift into human or other forms. In Japanese folklore the kitsune are considered to be messengers of Inari, the Shinto deity of rice, agriculture, and prosperity.

TRACKING DOWN CLUES

So many different talents! So many sizes and shapes!

Nothing about fairies is simple, including their origins. Celtic mythology describes fairies as a separate race of beings who occupied the landscape before human invasion. They were said to have used stone tools, some of which they left behind, but were defeated by the iron weapons of the Celts. Today we know more about the prehistoric peoples of Britain. To a farmer plowing a field long ago, however, the discovery of stone arrowheads hinted at strangers from an unknown world. Could those vanished creatures have been some kind of fairies?

Another set of clues lies in the connections between fairies and the natural world. Fairies explained all sorts of frightening squeaks, creaks, shadows, and shapes. An owl's screech could be interpreted as a banshee's wail. The branches of a dead tree could be the outstretched arms of a marsh-dwelling ballybog. A glowworm might be a will-o'-the-wisp, leading travelers astray with its ghostly, flickering light. On the darker side a baby suffering from an unusual illness or birth defect could be explained as a changeling left behind by fairies. This cruel line of reasoning would sometimes be used to justify mistreatment of the child.

More recent incarnations of fairies link to a different aspect of the natural world — the realm of Insecta, especially butterflies and dragonflies. Insect-like wings distinguish fairies from angels, who are usually shown with feathered wings like birds. Insects inspire fairy lore in many ways: They are flight experts that mastered the air some 150 million years before other flying animals. Insects were nature's first singers, too, communicating in a wide range of sounds, rhythms, and tones. Like fairies, they inhabit the world of flowers.

The mythologies of fairies have varied widely through time and across the globe. It's hard to pin the origins of these delightful nature spirits to any particular source — but that doesn't stop us from wanting them to be real.

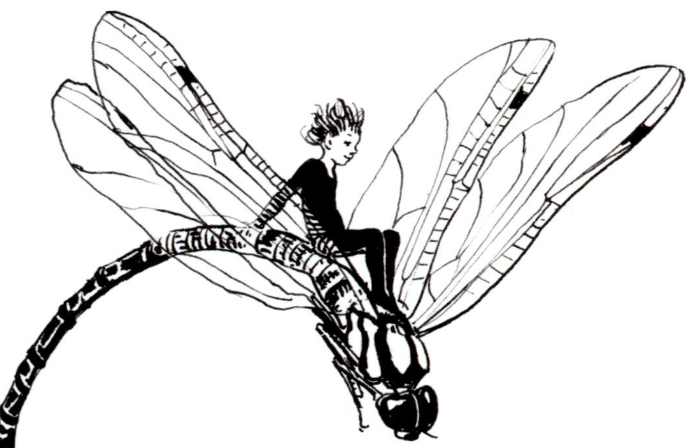

When the first baby laughed for the first time, its laugh broke into a thousand pieces, and they all went skipping about, and that was the beginning of fairies.

—J. M. Barrie, **Peter Pan**, 1911

The Fairy Queen on her chariot drawn by butterflies (illustration by Richard Doyle, 1846).

Fast and Fierce

Like fairies, dragonflies are colorful, fast, and fierce. Equipped with four glittering iridescent wings, they can fly in all directions, hover like helicopters, and reach speeds over thirty miles per hour. Dragonflies are among the world's most accurate hunters, succeeding in 90 percent of their attacks on mosquitoes and other prey.

You may think of dragonflies as speedy but harmless insects that live near rivers, ponds, and lakes. Travel back three hundred million years in time, however, and you'd find a more terrifying version. Back then, higher oxygen levels allowed insects to grow to enormous sizes. Imagine a dragonfly with a two-foot wingspan! That's the size of a hawk . . . or a good-sized fairy.

Fairy Circles

What causes mushrooms to grow in a circle like this? Traditional tales from Europe describe rings left by fairies dancing at night. A less magical explanation is that some types of fungus grow underground by sending out small threads, called mycelium, in a circular shape. In late summer to early autumn, the mushrooms pop out of the ground. Presto, a fairy circle.

Elf-Shot

In British folklore, elf-shot or elf-bolts were stone arrowheads produced by vanished peoples of prehistoric times. A cow seized with sudden illness was said to be the target of a fairy's arrow. People could be hit too, causing sharp pain in parts of the body. The victim of the attack was said to be "elf-struck"—a term that might have led to the modern medical term for a stroke. This arrowhead charm consists of a leaf-shaped flint arrowhead set in a crystal container bound with gold.

TO BE A FAIRY

Could a tiny flying humanoid ever exist?

Let's set aside supernatural talents like invisibility or shape-shifting. Yes, I know those are some of the best fairy traits! We'll still have plenty of challenges, though, figuring out how a creature of our world could (1) get very small, (2) go airborne, and (3) remain humanlike and lovely, as any self-respecting fairy would be.

First, the issue of size. With griffins we saw how the solid bones and stocky bodies of large mammals pose problems for flight. But a fairy is small, right? Turns out that no human species has ever been that adorably tiny. Nope! Not a single one since the earliest humans began walking upright on two legs over six million years ago. The smallest known humans — *Homo floresiensis*, a species that lived from around 190,000 to 50,000 years ago on the Indonesian island of Flores — stood just over three feet tall.

So why haven't humans ever evolved smaller bodies? Nobody really knows. Maybe our large brains require a minimum size to pack in all those essential nerve cells. Tiny humans would have a higher proportion of surface area to mass too, causing them to lose too much heat. They would likely have problems with breathing and blood circulation. Then there's the prospect of a whole new array of predators waiting to gobble a mini-person snack. (My childhood cat is coming to mind . . .)

Okay, it's true that some mammals are extremely small. Certain species of bats, for example. They're fliers with huge lung capacities, oversized hearts, light and long bones, and front limbs adapted into wings. But do you know any bats that look remotely like humans?

But there is a different creature to consider. At the University of Texas at Austin, Dr. Julia Clarke studies the evolution of birds and their ancestors, the theropod dinosaurs. Her work shows how birds are similar to humans in several ways. Birds are bipedal, standing upright like us. They are intelligent too, with nerve cells packed tightly together inside their little heads.

One bird in particular might be closest to fairy-hood. It's tiny and fierce — a glittering, jewellike gymnast that hovers and swoops, sipping sweet nectar from flowers. It's got no arms, but who needs those when you've got super-powered wings and a pointy, daggerlike beak?

It's a hummingbird!

The greater mouse-eared bat measures three inches from head to tail.

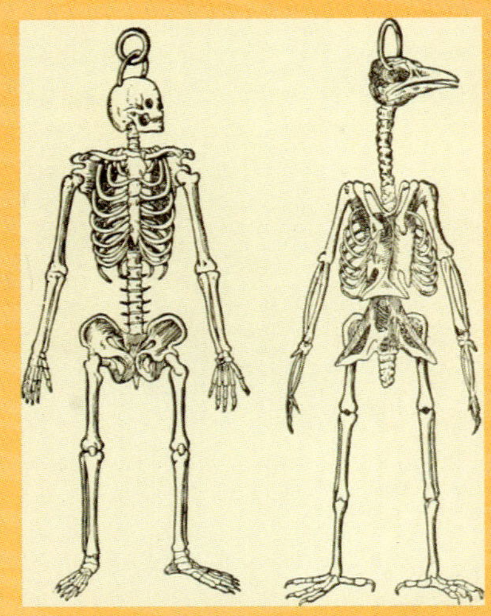

This image from 1555 compares the skeletons of a person and a bird drawn to the same scale. Humans and birds are both tetrapods—vertebrate animals with four limbs. Birds have evolved mostly hollow bones and other features that enable flight.

The bee hummingbird, the world's smallest bird, reaches 2.5 inches long.

Inventing Fairies

In 1917 two young cousins named Elsie and Frances produced photographs of fairies they claimed to have seen near their home in Cottingley, England. The public seized on the "Cottingley Fairies" as evidence of a mystical world—a welcome relief from the miseries of war then raging in Europe. One prominent supporter was Sir Arthur Conan Doyle, author of the famous Sherlock Holmes stories.

Encouraged, the girls took more photographs. To our eyes their efforts might look clumsy; it's obvious now that the figures were cut out of paper and fastened to the ground with pins. Yet the cousins stuck to their story for over sixty years. In 1981 Frances finally admitted that four of the five pictures were faked. The fifth one, she insisted, was real.

The Stolen Child

Come away, O human child!
To the waters and the wild
With a faery, hand in hand,
For the world's more full of weeping than you
can understand.

—William Butler Yeats, 1886

A fairy house, built for the tiniest and most magical neighbors.

The clurichaun of Irish lore, mischievous cousin of the leprechaun (T. C. Croker, 1892).

Many legends warn of the increasing separation between humans and fairies, as we become less connected to the natural world. Yet fairies remain with us — mischievous, enchanting, and ready to enliven many stories to come.

We'll soar higher now, with another mythical creature of the air. Prepare for the fiery flight of a most remarkable bird.

PHOENIX
The Fire Bird

LET'S IMAGINE . . .

A boy looks over the rising floodwaters of the Nile River from a rooftop in ancient Egypt, around 3,500 years ago. Smoke rises in tendrils from cooking fires nearby. Behind him the boy's mother unfolds sleeping mats woven from palm fronds. The season of *akhet* has barely begun, but already it's too hot to sleep inside.

"What's that?" The boy points to a huge, long-necked bird overhead. Its broad wings catch the burning red glow of sunset. A crest of black feathers adorns its head. The bird flaps a slow, steady beat as it travels the green riverbank.

"Oh, a great heron!" cries his mother. "I haven't seen one in years."

Together they watch the bird disappear into the purple-red horizon.

"Where is it going?" asks the boy. "To find Papa's ship?"

"That would be a long journey." The mother smiles, but tears fill her eyes.

Her son leans against her. "But the bird is strong — did you see how big it was?"

"The biggest of all." She strokes the boy's hair. "They say that the great heron lives far to the East, in a beautiful garden with a tall tree for its nest and a pool of clear water below, so sweet that the sun god stops every day to drink. Once in a great while the bird leaves its home and travels far down the river to begin a new life."

"Papa will see it then, from his ship," murmurs the boy.

"Perhaps. You can ask him, when he returns to us. Come, it's time to sleep."

The boy lies down. The sounds of evening gather over him like a blanket — the voices of neighbors, the clinking of pots, the lullaby that his mother hums. He closes his eyes and drifts, smelling the cooking fires and the deep, rich scent of mud from the river. Sleep finds him, and he dreams of nests and wings, of smoke and sky and a fabulous sunbird, born of fire . . .

the phoenix.

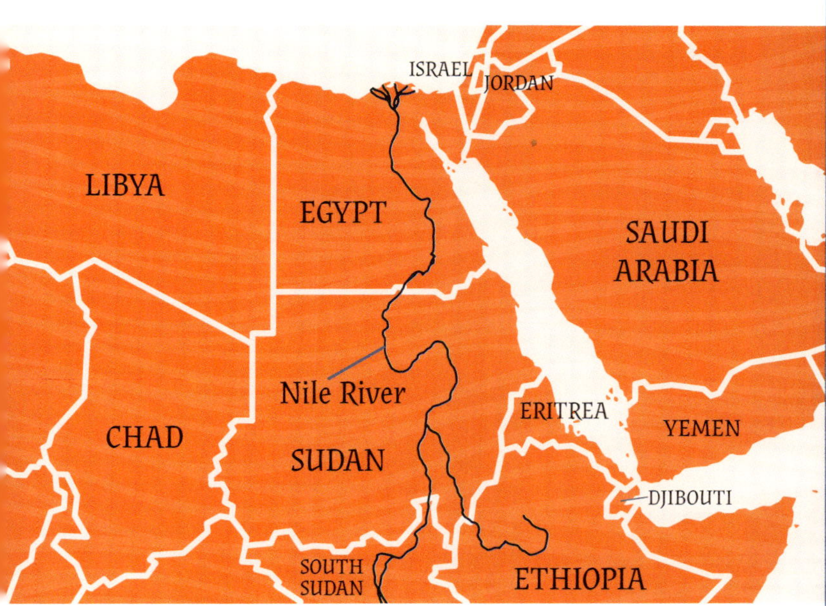

GIFT OF THE NILE

When astronauts look down at Earth, they can see a green ribbon winding through the desert of northern Africa. That's the Nile River. It flows south to north over four thousand miles and through eleven countries before emptying into the Mediterranean Sea.

The civilization of ancient Egypt, often called the "gift of the Nile," flourished along this great waterway for over three thousand years. The river flooded every summer, watering the crops and replenishing the soil. Traders and travelers used the river to move between Upper Egypt in the south and Lower Egypt to the north. All kinds of wildlife inhabited the river corridor, especially birds. Millions of birds migrated between Europe and Africa. Others found homes in marshes and wetlands. These ecosystems remain important to bird populations today.

Life along the Nile connected the people of ancient Egypt to nature's cycles of change and renewal. The river determined their calendar. The season of inundation, *akhet*, took place during the annual floods from June to September, followed by the growing season (*peret*) and harvest time (*shemu*). Nature inspired beautiful artwork depicting animals and plants. Many Egyptian gods took on animallike features—cats, lions, cows, even crocodiles and baboons. Birds played a big role too. The great sun god, Ra, wore the head of a falcon. The goddess Isis was often shown with wings. From these traditions the magnificent mythical phoenix arose.

Ra with a raven head.

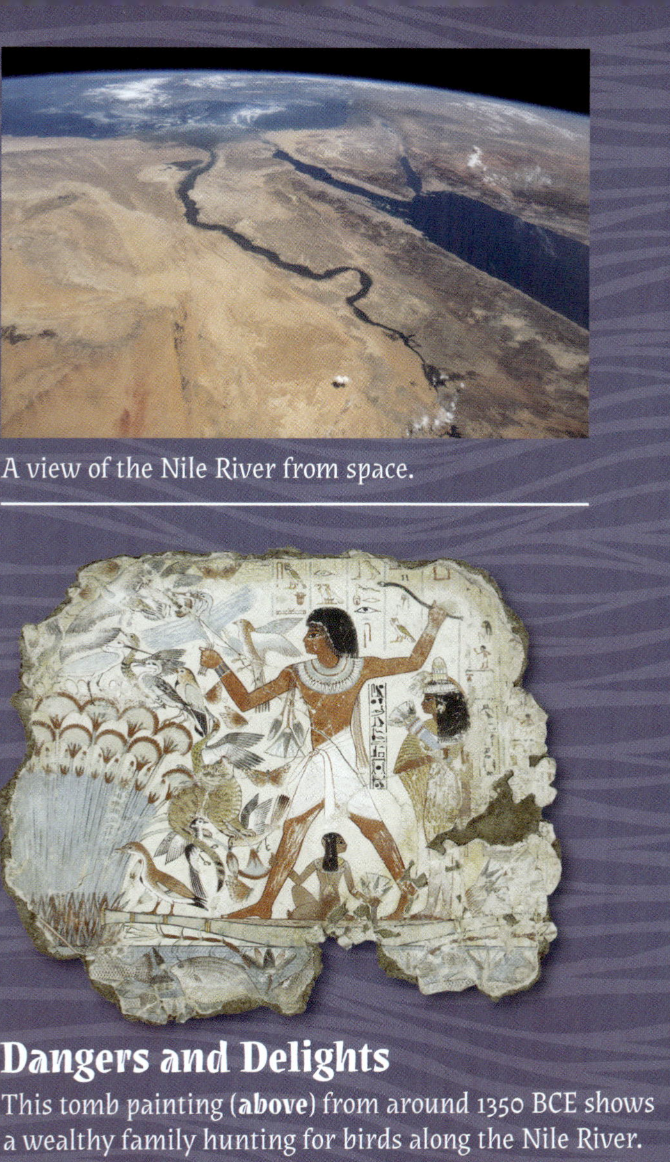

A view of the Nile River from space.

Dangers and Delights

This tomb painting (**above**) from around 1350 BCE shows a wealthy family hunting for birds along the Nile River. Dangers lurked along the river too, like crocodiles and poisonous snakes. Hippos were feared for their aggressive habits of charging and capsizing boats. The lotus painted on the hippo statue (**below**) represents rebirth, as the flowers of a lotus close at night and reopen when the sun comes up.

LEGENDS AND LORE

Magical, radiant, shimmering! With flowing plumage of orange, purple, red, and gold, the phoenix embodies the powerful energy of the sun. Its eyes shine like sapphires. Its tears heal any injury. Unique among animals, the phoenix possesses the power to renew itself and thereby live forever.

According to legends from ancient Egypt, only one phoenix existed in the world at one time. It dwelt in paradise, a land of infinite beauty lying beyond the horizon toward Arabia and the rising sun. Every five hundred years or so, as the phoenix felt its end approaching, it built a mound of cinnamon twigs and fragrant resin atop the Temple of the Sun God in Heliopolis, Egypt. There it burst into flames and expired in a blaze of glory and ashes. It left behind one last flickering spark, from which a new, fully grown phoenix emerged into the cool starlight.

Immortal bird, spicy nest, fiery explosions! What's not to like? The Greeks and Romans adopted this sizzling story from the Egyptians — though not without a few adjustments. Pliny the Elder, for example, questioned the claim that the ashes of a phoenix could bring a dead person back to life. What good was that, he scoffed, if the cure is available just once every five hundred years?

Nevertheless, the legend of the phoenix continued to flourish, reborn in new places and times. The Greeks bestowed the bird with its name — the word φοινιξ, pronounced "FOY-nix," meaning the color purple-red or crimson. Sometime around 118 CE the Romans minted gold coins featuring the head of Emperor Trajan on one side and a phoenix on the other, crowned with a halolike nimbus. Early Christians embraced the phoenix as a symbol of the death and resurrection of Jesus.

The phoenix's popularity reached new heights during the European Renaissance of the fifteenth and sixteenth centuries. Named after the French word for "rebirth," this period celebrated a revival of ideas and achievement from classical Greece and Rome. What a boost for the phoenix! Viewed now as a myth rather than a real animal, the fiery bird swooped into a vast array of sonnets, love poems, epithets, and epic tales. William Shakespeare mentioned it in nine of his famous plays.

More recently we celebrate the phoenix as a trusty companion of wizards, the namesake of cities, and, as always, an enduring symbol of hope and rebirth after destruction. Cheer up! A new era is about to begin.

Phoenix rising from the ashes, in **Book of Mythological Creatures**, 1806.

Roman gold coins, c. 117 CE.

Bird of Creation: The Sacred Bennu

In creation myths of ancient Egypt, the great Bennu bird flew over the waters of chaos before the world began. It flew for a long time. Finally, with a last flap and a glide, the bird folded its huge wings to land on a rock. From there it called out over the vast empty expanse, singing the world into creation and marking the beginning of time.

The Bennu deity of Egyptian mythology offers clues to the phoenix legend. The sacred bird embodied the **ba**, or soul, of the sun god, Ra. It served as companion to Osiris, god of the immortal dead, and represented the cyclical flooding of the Nile. The sacred bird appears in the Egyptian **Book of the Dead**—the ritual spells inscribed on papyrus to help the deceased find their way to the afterlife. The Bennu looks like a heron, a type of wading bird with long legs and a curvy neck. It is depicted wearing the White Crown of Osiris . . . and it looks suspiciously like many images of the phoenix. Hail to the sacred Bennu!

A Magical Flock

Divine birds arise in mythologies across the world. Each emerges from a separate tradition and presents distinct features. In China the fenghuang (**below left**) symbolizes the empress and reigns over all other birds. Its body expresses the five Chinese virtues—goodness, duty, propriety, kindness, and reliability—and its name represents the union of yin-yang, or male and female. The fenghuang lives forever but appears only in times of peace and prosperity.

The firebird of Russian folklore (**center**) heals the sick with its song and drops pearls from its beak at each note. It lives on golden apples, which might explain its sparkling eyes and glowing plumage. From Persia comes the simurgh (**right**), often depicted as an enormous peacock. While fierce in appearance, the simurgh is kind and wise. Sometimes, as shown here, it even provides a handy rescue to stranded heroes.

TRACKING DOWN CLUES

Time for a recap. We've seen that the mythical phoenix bears a strong mythical resemblance to the sacred Bennu, the ancient Egyptian deity linked with the sun, creation, and rebirth. And the deity looks a lot like an oversized heron. It's got all the right parts — the long, skinny legs, the curvy neck, the sharp beak.

One problem: The sacred Bennu is much bigger than any heron alive today. Were ancient Egyptians simply inspired to draw massive versions of herons living along the Nile River? Or was there another possible influence?

Enter the now-extinct *Ardea bennuides*, otherwise known as the great or Bennu heron (an actual bird, not the one wearing a big hat). In the 1970s Danish archaeologist Dr. Ella Hoch discovered fossils of an enormous heron on the island of Umm an-Nar in the United Arab Emirates. Based on estimates, the bird may have had a nine-foot wingspan and a height up to seven feet. That's taller than the goliath heron, the world's largest living species, which reaches five feet high at the most.

From further scientific findings we know that this giant bird lived during ancient Egyptian times. From its home on the Arabian Peninsula, *Ardea bennuides* may have winged its way to the Nile River, flying from the east with the sun. Like all herons, it would hang out in wetlands and marshes, ready to stab a passing fish for dinner. But it was a rare bird, seldom seen and soon to go extinct. That elusive quality may have added to the belief that only one phoenix existed at a time.

With help from the fossil record, a picture begins to emerge: A visiting heron might be spotted by someone, perhaps a family on a rooftop. They watch the bird flap its huge wings. They see it land on a rock and stand alone, surrounded by floodwaters. Sunlight glints on the bird's feathers — red, purple, gold! — and a timeless myth catches fire.

REPRESENTATION OF THE BENNU.
(*From a Ritual.*)

"I am the Bennu bird, the Heart-Soul of Ra, the Guide of the Gods to the Duat [Underworld]."

—Egyptian Book of the Dead

High-Flying Herons

Several species of heron make their home or travel along the Nile River today. Gray herons (**above left**), common during the winter season, build their nests in treetops as the mythical phoenix was said to do. Purple herons (**above right**) also rest in high places during the flood season. Goliath herons are the largest living member of the family. But the now-extinct Bennu heron (**right**)—represented here by its mythical counterpart, the sacred Bennu—would have stood two feet taller. Legend-worthy!

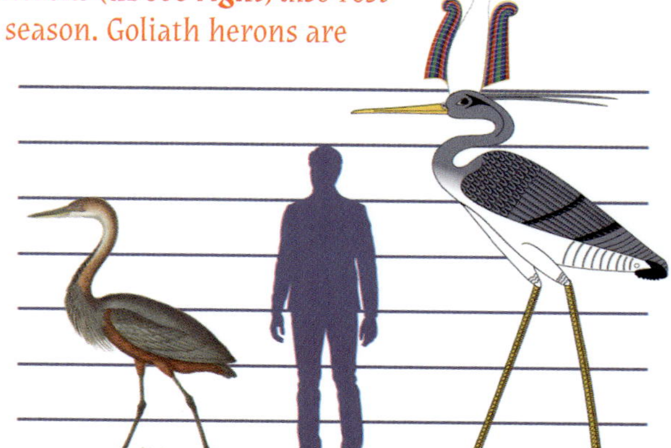

Don't Forget the Cat!

Ancient Egyptians were obsessed with the afterlife. To prepare, they mummified bodies and stacked tombs with the essentials of daily life, including furniture, jewelry, clothing . . . and animals. Cats, crocodiles, dogs, snakes, hawks, ibis, mongooses, even lion cubs! They applied the highest skills to mummifying animals, whether intended as sacrifices to the gods or animal companions for the deceased person. These mummies provide insights into relationships between ancient people and the animals that shared their lives.

Grounded

Seven hundred years ago Arab traders told of the roc, a huge bird that could lift an elephant into the sky. Sailors claimed that the terrifying predator inhabited an island off the southern coast of Africa. The roc became a popular topic in folktales . . . but was it only a story?

In the nineteenth century, on the island country of Madagascar off the southeast coast of Africa, fossil hunters discovered remains of **Aepyornis**, or elephant bird. This supersized monster once stood over ten feet tall and laid two-gallon-sized eggs. Could this be proof of a real live roc? One minor issue, however: Aepyornis was much too big and heavy to fly.

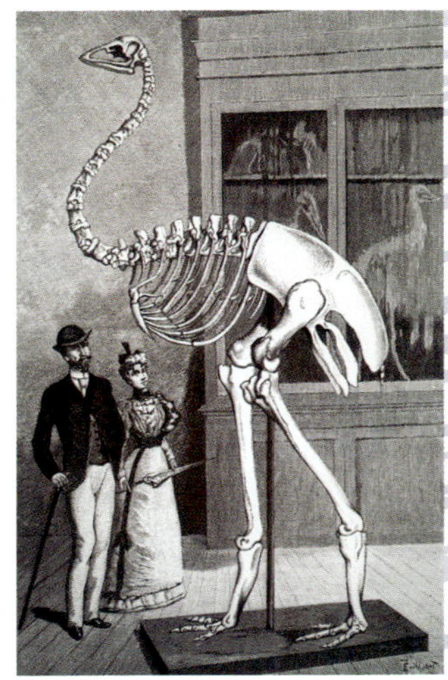

Elephant birds.

TO BE A PHOENIX

Prepare to challenge the laws of physics!

According to legend, the phoenix follows certain steps to ensure its immortal state. After five hundred blissful years in paradise, the mythical beast gets restless and decides to build a funerary nest. First it gathers a pile of dry, fragrant plants like sandalwood, cinnamon, and juniper. Then it climbs on top.

What happens next?

Let's look at what happens when things burn up. Fire is the visible manifestation of a chemical reaction called combustion. It requires three components: fuel, heat, and oxygen. No problem! The nest is ready and there's plenty of fresh air, composed of about 21 percent oxygen. A quick spark, courtesy of the sun god . . . IGNITION! The fuel (one senior-citizen phoenix on its comfy perch) combines with oxygen and undergoes combustion, releasing water vapor and the odorless, colorless gas called carbon dioxide.

Flames soar! Branches crackle! Embers glow!

Now back to the phoenix. A bird might not be as easily combustible as a pile of twigs, but the temperature's going up. Soon it'll catch fire too, and disappear into the inferno before emerging to start life over again. Right?

Except . . . wait. The roaring fire is giving off more than smoke and flames. It's releasing energy — the phoenix's energy. This energy radiates outward as a hot blast. The bonfire is obeying a basic law of science, called the first law of thermodynamics. This states that energy cannot be created or destroyed, but it can move from a system (in this case, the phoenix) to the surroundings through the transfer of heat. That's definitely happening! The area around the fire is blazing hot! Soon all that's left is a pile of ashes, including unburnt fragments of bones and beak.

Could a bird pull itself back together from hot air and a pile of ashes?

Fortunately for phoenix fans, legends don't rely on the laws of science. For thousands of years this immortal bird has symbolized rejuvenation and rebirth. Its story sustained ancient Egyptians through droughts, invasions, hardships, and upheavals. The mythical phoenix will endure, ready to rise again as an ever-inspiring messenger of hope.

The Case of the Immortal Jellyfish

Possible loophole! Maybe there's a way to live forever . . . if you're willing to be a jellyfish.

Most jellyfish begin life as larva that mature into branching polyps and then young, free-floating jellyfish. The mature jellyfish, or medusas, produce eggs and the cycle begins again. The immortal jellyfish, however, use a strategy that scientists call the "phoenix cycle." When a medusa of this type of jellyfish is damaged, it sinks to the ocean floor and begins to decay. Amazingly, its cells then reorganize into polyps and produce brand new jellyfish. The same exact cells have reverted into babies! (Well, the jellyfish equivalent of babies.) The immortal jellyfish has reversed the aging process and found a way to live forever.

Danger from Above!

We think of birds as songsters, colorful fliers, or, like the phoenix, symbols of magical realms. But not all birds are friendly. Early in human history birds were often the predators while we were the prey. The Taung Child fossil (**below right**) from South Africa belongs to a prehistoric human species called **Australopithecus africanus** that lived 2.6 million years ago. Close study of the skull shows scratches and holes in the eye sockets. These marks were probably inflicted when a large bird carried off the child, who was about three years old. Today monkeys that are preyed upon by African crowned eagles show the same pattern of injury.

Egyptian goddess Isis.

Since before written history humans have revered birds for their powers of flight. We've worshipped them as deities, feared them as predators, and hunted them to extinction. In every part of the world we've celebrated them in stories.

What might happen if we combined an extraordinary bird and a powerful serpent into a single, awe-inspiring creature? We'll leave the ancient civilization of Egypt and travel to the Americas to find out.

QUETZALCOATL
The Feathered Serpent

LET'S IMAGINE . . .

In the mountains of what is now Guatemala, some 2,500 years ago, a girl and her younger brother make their way up a trail. The cloud forest hums with life — the trilling of frogs, the chitter of insects, the whooping barks of howler monkeys. The morning sky is blue, but soon fog will tumble down the ridge and be caught among the trees. All will be misty again.

The children move quickly, alert to signs of a jaguar or snake. They duck under vines of bright pink orchids. They gather avocados and snails. Sunlight warms their backs, and the mossy forest floor silences their steps. The siblings enter a grove of avocado trees — and halt.

On a branch a gray-green bird lifts its head in a soft, warbling song. The boy raises his blowgun to shoot, but his sister stops him. *Wait,* she signals. Listen. For a moment, the forest seems to hold its breath. Water drips from leaves with a quiet *plop-plop-plop*. The river rumbles in the distance. Beetles and millipedes rustle underfoot.

Suddenly, a bigger bird with an impossibly long tail bursts from the shadows. *Wacka-wacka-wacka!* it calls, raucous and loud. It spirals upward, tail feathers undulating like a fast-moving snake. Sunlight glitters on its iridescent green and red feathers, brilliant and shimmering. Soon it is a speck overhead, a glint of color. Finally it swivels and dives to disappear into the trees.

"Is it bird," whispers the boy, "or snake?"

His sister doesn't answer. She's watching something fall from the sky: a tail feather torn loose by the creature's rushing flight. It twists in the breeze, drifts closer, and settles at their feet. The girl picks it up — a feather longer than her arm, sparkling turquoise and copper and deep fern green. The gift of a bird that flies like a snake. The one who would be known as the feathered serpent —

Quetzalcoatl.

MYSTERIES OF MESOAMERICA

For nearly three thousand years a rich array of cultures flourished in the lands of Central America and Mexico — the area we call Mesoamerica. These cultures built magnificent cities with palaces, temples, and street grids aligned with the stars. They invented intricate systems of writing, mathematics, and timekeeping. They traded goods and fought fierce battles. Through peacetime or war, the different peoples of Mesoamerica shared several customs and beliefs, from the popular ball game known as *tlachtli* to the rituals of human sacrifice practiced by some groups.

Archaeological discoveries reveal that many civilizations rose and declined in Mesoamerica through the centuries. The first major culture, known as the Olmecs, thrived from 1600 to 350 BCE along the Gulf Coast. The Olmecs left behind distinctive sculptures of immense stone heads. Farther south, the Maya civilization began its long history around 1500 BCE, with a highpoint of ancient culture around 500 CE. Maya people still live in these regions today.

The powerful Aztecs, who called themselves Mexica, arrived at the Valley of Mexico around 1250 CE. Here they encountered a mystery: an immense ruined city lying northeast of their new home. Who built this great place . . . and what had happened to them? The Aztecs revered the mysterious city as a sacred place. They named it Teotihuacán, meaning "the place of the gods" in their Nahuatl language.

The mysteries of Teotihuacán endure today. Ruins cover some eight square miles, evidence of the ambitious, vanished people who built America's first metropolis almost two thousand years ago. Visitors can stroll for more than a mile down the Avenue of the Dead, past the Pyramids of the Moon and Sun. At the heart of the city they can climb the steep steps of a smaller temple to find carvings of seashells, snakes, and giant grinning heads — the Pyramid of the Feathered Serpent.

LEGENDS AND LORE

He was a bird-snake. A priestly king. The god of wind, patron of civilization, benevolent and life-bringing deity.

While some Mesoamerican gods were believed to require human flesh and blood to sustain themselves, Quetzalcoatl was thought to oppose human sacrifice. His popularity expanded over the centuries as he took on ever-changing roles and names. The Maya called him Kukulcan and built a sacred pyramid in his honor sometime around 1000 CE. The Toltec people, who dominated central Mexico from 900 to 1150 CE, venerated him as god of the planet Venus, often called the star of morning and evening. His temple formed the center of their capital city of Tula. Artists began to depict him in human form.

In the tenth century a Toltec priest took the name Topiltzin Quetzalcoatl, meaning "Our Young Prince the Plumed Serpent." The empire prospered under his wise rule. The prince ran into trouble, however, when he wanted to replace human sacrifices with offerings of butterflies and lizards. Rival priests rebelled. Surely, they insisted, the gods required the brave, beating hearts of captive warriors! According to legend, the priestly prince Topiltzin fled to the eastern coast and sailed away on a raft of snakes, promising to return.

The Aztecs (Mexicas) revered Quetzalcoatl as a god of creation. Like many Mesoamerican cultures, they believed that the cosmos undergoes cycles of creation and destruction. Their mythology tells of four previous ages — or cycles of suns — each destroyed by a cataclysm of flood, earthquake, hurricane, or fire. Through these upheavals Quetzalcoatl battled other gods to restore humankind.

After the last disaster the mythical hero Quetzalcoatl gathered the scattered bones of the ancient dead, ground them up, and mixed them with his own blood to form new human bodies. Then he changed himself into a black ant, crawled underground, and brought back corn so the people would survive. He gifted them with the sacred calendar, too, as well as the arts of writing, education, and craftsmanship. In these ways Quetzalcoatl brought civilization to the age of the fifth sun — the world we inhabit today.

And when the wind rose, when the dust rumbled, and it crackled and there was a great din . . . then it was said: Quetzalcoatl is wrathful.

—**The Florentine Codex**, compiled by Friar Bernardino de Sahagún (c. 1569)

A Guardian Deity

This Olmec sculpture may be the earliest depiction of a creature related to Quetzalcoatl. Crafted roughly three thousand years ago, it shows a serpent with a feathered crest curved protectively around a man. Together they face a common enemy.

Shapeshifter of Many Names

Aztec images often show Quetzalcoatl as a rattlesnake with feathers. As the god of wind, known as Ehécatl, he typically wears a conical hat, an elaborate headdress, and a red duck-billed mask that blows forth the wind.

Rivalry of Brothers

Like many of us Quetzalcoatl didn't always get along with his siblings. His "evil twin" was Tezcatlipoca—creator and destroyer, omnipotent god of rulers, sorcerers, and warriors. To the Aztecs their rivalry represented a balance of opposing powers. Sometimes the brothers fought, with the feathered serpent pitted against Tezcatlipoca's black jaguar. In other myths they joined to create earth and sky by ripping apart a reptilian monster. The monster could be heard at night, screaming for human hearts. If fed, she would continue to grow crops from her body. This belief underlaid the practice of human sacrifice, a common ritual among followers of Tezcatlipoca.

This ceremonial Aztec mask of Tezcatlipoca was crafted with mosaics of turquoise and shell. Black stripes encircle Tezcatlipoca's head, with mosaic glued onto a human skull—complete with movable jaw.

Bird of Power

Mythical birds exist in many Indigenous American traditions. One of the most famous, the thunderbird, swoops through legends in the Pacific Northwest, Great Lakes, and other regions. The thunderbird could pluck a whale from the ocean, it was said. Its wings blew thunderstorms, and a blink of its eyes sent lightning jagging down from the sky.

Eagle on a Cactus

Another bird-serpent duo played a role in Mesoamerican history. Remember the Aztecs, who discovered the ruins of Teotihuacán? Before arriving in the Valley of Mexico around 1250, they'd been wandering for two hundred years in search of a new home. A prophecy guided them—the belief that someday they would come upon a giant eagle with a snake in its beak, perched on a cactus. At that spot they were destined to build a great city.

On a swampy island in Lake Texcoco, at modern-day Mexico City, the prophecy came true. Here the Aztecs built Tenochtitlan, a new capital city distinguished by monumental buildings, ambitious causeways and irrigation canals, and islands called chinampas that produced enormous crops of squash, corn, and beans. They conquered neighboring city-states and demanded tributes of cocoa beans, feathers, precious metals, and human captives. When Spanish conquistadors arrived in 1519, the Aztec Empire included some five million people.

Despite their power and wealth, the Aztecs quickly succumbed to high-powered weaponry and devastating diseases brought by the Spanish invaders. Tenochtitlan fell in 1521. The last great ancient civilization of Mesoamerica came to an end—yet the eagle on a cactus adorns the proud flag of Mexico today.

TRACKING DOWN CLUES

For a shortcut to Quetzalcoatl's identity take a look at the name. In the Nahuatl language of the Aztecs (Mexicas), *quetzal* means "precious feather" and *cóatl* means "snake." Bird + snake = feathered serpent.

The Maya and Aztecs loved to use feathers to decorate ceremonial clothing, capes, and artwork. Royal palaces kept cages of brightly colored parrots, hummingbirds, and macaws to supply the feather-works industry. The most coveted feathers, however, came from a bird that didn't thrive in captivity: the resplendent quetzal bird.

Quetzals live in cloud forests — high-altitude rainforests known for dreamlike mists, fast rivers, and moss-covered trees. With brilliant green backs and white bellies splashed with crimson red, they rank among the most beautiful of birds. And it gets better! During the mating season a male resplendent quetzal grows iridescent green tail feathers that reach up to three feet long. He shows these off to a potential mate by spiraling upward into the sky. The wavelike motion of his magnificent train makes the bird look eerily like a snake.

With such unique plumage it's no wonder that the bird caught the attention of Maya people of the highland forests. They gathered quetzal tail feathers by trapping the males at watering spots and nests, probably using nets or sticky resins. Then they released the birds and waited for the long plumes to grow back the next year. The quetzal was considered to be sacred, and killing even a single bird brought the penalty of death. Only certain people were allowed to capture them; that right was inherited and brought great wealth to those who obtained feathers for trade. Codices recorded how the Aztec rulers received large quantities of quetzal feathers from the south, delivered as tribute from conquered tribes. Today the resplendent quetzal is increasingly rare due to loss of habitat and illegal trade.

The Aztecs revered snakes, too, as guardian creatures linked to energies of the earth. Rattlesnakes were among the fiercest, and were often portrayed in sculptures, mosaics, and other artwork. Together the resplendent quetzal bird and the powerful serpent joined as the mythical Quetzalcoatl of Mesoamerica, uniting the airy province of sky with the earthly realm.

Resplendent quetzal bird.

Basilisk rattlesnake.

Although it be gold,
it is crushed,
Although it be quetzal
feather, it is torn asunder.
Not forever on earth;
only a little while here.

—Nezahualcóyotl,
Warrior-Poet of Texcoco (b. 1402)

An Aztec artist carved this coiled rattlesnake with realistic details of fangs, bifurcated tongue, and segmented tail.

"Montezuma's Headdress"

Only the most powerful Aztec rulers or priests were allowed to wear garments adorned with quetzal feathers. This famous headdress might have belonged to Emperor Montezuma II.

A People in Pictures

The Aztec people recorded their lives and beliefs in manuscripts called codices. A codex is a special type of book created on a long strip of tree bark or deerskin that folds up like an accordion. Colorful pictures and symbols describe historical events, royal family relationships, religious ceremonies, and accounts of payments and tributes.

Spanish priests destroyed most of the Aztec codices after the conquest in 1521. Luckily, a handful survived. Codices from the pre-Columbian era (before arrival of Europeans) contain pictographs and symbols used by the Aztecs, like these pages of the **Codex Borbonicus** from around 1520. After colonization, codices often included text in Spanish along with pictures. An example is the **Codex Tovar**, created in 1587 with an image of Quetzalcoatl in human form, wearing his characteristic pointed hat.

Codex Borbonicus (above).

Codex Tovar (left).

Serpent Mountain

At Templo Mayor (Main Temple) of the Aztec capital of Tenochtitlan, a set of menacing snake sculptures mark the base of a giant pyramid. Long ago unlucky victims would pass the serpents while climbing up to be sacrificed at the pyramid's top. Archaeologists believe the pyramid was built to honor a sacred place in Aztec history known as Coatepec, or Serpent Mountain. Today the temple is located in the heart of Mexico City. Its ruins, discovered in 1978, are visited by nearly a million people each year.

TO BE QUETZALCOATL

Here's a recipe for the legendary feathered serpent: In a sacred bowl, combine one part shimmering bird of the cloud forest with one part slithering snake. Add a sprinkle of jaguar, a pinch of eagle. Stir well. Throw in a healthy dose of human hero, wait for the world to end and begin again, and —

What's that? You can't wait that long?

Okay, let's consider other possibilities for combining a bird with a snake. Both types of animals descend from reptile ancestors that adapted to life on dry land around 320 million years ago. Since then lots has happened. Around 240 million years ago the animals we call archosaurs — ancestors of dinosaurs, pterosaurs, and crocodiles — branched off from other reptiles. Each of those groups continued to diverge into new family lines. One branch, called the Ornithodiran, included dinosaurs and pterosaurs. Dinosaurs went on to split into several lineages. One of those, the therapods (think T. rex!), gave rise to birds starting around 160 million years ago.

Which brings us to . . . feathers! The only animals to grow feather-like structures belong to the Ornithodiran group. And the last common ancestor shared by the Ornithodirans and the Squamata — reptiles like lizards and snakes — dates back to the early archosaurs. That's well over two hundred million years ago, and the two groups have been diverging ever since. In other words, no self-respecting serpent has ever grown a single feather.

And even if snakes could *grow* feathers, such poofy plumage would offer a serpentlike creature nothing but trouble. Feathers probably evolved to help dinosaurs attract mates. They also provided insulation. Cold-blooded animals such as snakes, however, need direct exposure to surrounding temperatures because they can't regulate their temperatures internally. Feathers would prevent a snake from warming in the sun or cooling off in the shade. They'd likely interfere with a snake's style of locomotion too. Imagine trying to slither when you're covered with fluff. And how would a snake keep those feathers clean?

Maybe things don't look so promising for bird-snake combinations in the natural world. Nevertheless, we can continue to celebrate Mesoamerica's feathered serpent — shape-shifting trickster of many names, patron and protector of people.

One day, we hope to turn their feathers into scales and get one step closer to creating a dinosaur-like chicken.

—Dr. Rory Cooper, developmental biologist at the University of Geneva

The sixteenth-century **Codex Laud** depicts Quetzalcoatl in two of his forms: feathered serpent and god of the wind. The manuscript was created on deerskin with covers of jaguar hide.

Quetzalcoatlus

For 150 million years, during the Age of Dinosaurs, pterosaurs ruled the skies over all of Earth's continents. They flew on wings made of skin, like bats. The smallest pterosaur measured no bigger than a pigeon, but the largest were the biggest flying animals that ever lived on Earth.

In 1971 a student at the University of Texas named Douglas Lawson discovered fossils of a huge pterosaur in Big Bend National Park near the Texas-Mexico border. Today you can see its replica at the park—**Quetzalcoatlus northropi**, named in honor of the Aztec feathered serpent and god of the wind. These amazing creatures stood twelve feet tall, with wingspans of about forty feet. (Remember the Bennu heron fossils of the United Arab Emirates, with their nine-foot wingspans? They were shrimps in comparison!)

Pterosaurs disappeared in the extinction that killed off the non-avian dinosaurs, sixty-six million years ago. But their fossils continue to surface. Could those ancient remains have influenced the Quetzalcoatl legend? It's unlikely, say experts. The fragile, thin-walled bones of pterosaurs are mostly hollow, like the bones of some birds. They tend to crush like a bag of potato chips, making it difficult to identify the animal's original form.

Sonic Hedgehog and the Chicken Legs

Over the last several years, a research team at the University of Geneva in Switzerland has been playing around with Sonic the Hedgehog. No, not the video game! They're experimenting with a gene that produces a protein molecule named Sonic Hedgehog, or SHH.

Genes are units of DNA within cells that determine how an organism will grow. The SHH gene acts like a messenger, signaling within and between cells in ways that affect many body structures. Variations of the gene help to determine whether certain types of animals will grow feathers, spines, scales, or fur on the skin. You've got hair, for example, while a hedgehog grows those prickly quills.

What does this have to do with Quetzalcoatl? Recently the scientists in Switzerland managed a breakthrough. By injecting a special solution into a chicken embryo in its egg, they activated the SHH gene and triggered the growth of feathers in spots on the legs where scales would normally form. Could this technology someday produce a scale-covered bird with fangs for a beak and plumes on its head? Draw a picture of that, please, and send it to me.

During Aztec times, this double-headed serpent probably served as a chest ornament. The mosaic consists of turquoise and red oyster shell, with conch shell for the teeth.

So far in these pages we've met birds of fire and guardians of gold. We've seen wind spirits, sea serpents, and giants of the land. Our next and last family of mythical wonders combines all of these features . . . and more.

Plus, they're really, really big.

Bring on the dragons!

LET'S IMAGINE . . .

A thousand years ago, in Southern Africa, the village girls chatter as they fetch water. It's the rainy season, and tall green grasses sway in the breeze. The girls tip their jugs into the cool stream. Then one of them screams. She points to the opposite bank, where an enormous python coils around the body of a crocodile. Jaws wide, eyes glinting, the monster snake gulps down its prey, inch by inch.

Five hundred years later a boy takes a shortcut down the beach of what is now southwest England. Storms have battered the coastline for weeks, and he's eager to get home before the next rainstorm hits. He trips over a boulder . . . and stops. This is no ordinary rock. It's the stone-hard skull of a massive beast with razor-sharp teethlike daggers. The boy steps away from the bones. He stares out to sea. What other terrible creatures are alive out there, under the dark waves?

Two hundred years ago, in a town of eastern China, a family prepares for the Lunar New Year. Red lanterns hang from the rafters of their home. Scrolls decorate the well-scrubbed walls. From the kitchen come fragrant smells of dumplings, roast duck, and cakes. Amid the bustle a small girl slips into her grandfather's quiet studio. His polished desk gleams in the dim light.

The old man looks up. "What is it, little one?"

The girl opens her fist to offer a sticky treat of bean paste and sesame. "Could you tell me a story, Grandfather, before the parade? The one about the boy and the pearl?"

He smiles and lays down his brush. "Well, since you brought such a fine gift. All right. In a time of hunger, a boy found a pearl under the grass in a secret valley. And what happens next?"

"He swallowed the pearl. And then they had plenty of rice."

"Correct. More importantly, the boy turned into — "

"Yeye, I hear the drums!" The girl takes his hand as sound fills the air. She helps him through the courtyard and front hall, out to the street. Everyone is there, dressed in their finest robes. Horns blare. Banners wave. Incense swirls and firecrackers pop. Dancers sway toward them, holding the great serpent aloft. Its huge head dips and turns, bearded and grinning, chasing a pearl —

the dragon.

The Book of Marvels

Marco Polo claimed to have seen dragons while traveling across the steppes of central Asia to China around 1300 CE. A century later, in France, **The Book of Marvels of the World** included his reports in a collection of illustrated tales.

A thousand years ago this Korean dragon decorated the rafters of a Buddhist temple or royal hall.

A FASCINATION WITH DRAGONS

They're jumbo-sized, reptilian, and ferocious. They show up in mythologies across the globe, from the tropical jungles to ice-bound islands. Why are we so obsessed with dragons?

One theory is that dragons represent our most powerful predators. In many parts of Africa, where our species originated around three hundred thousand years ago, snakes are a common and often dangerous part of life. Perhaps the fear of snakes began as a survival strategy and persisted as people spread across the globe. There's even a word for an extreme form of that fear of serpents: "ophidiophobia," a condition shared by about 10 percent of adults and 20 percent of teenagers today.

Next let's add a few more predators alongside the reptiles, such as raptor birds and big cats like leopards and tigers. Yikes! Now we have an excellent assortment of creatures most likely to kill us. We've also got all the essential parts that go into making a dragon. (For winged Western dragons, I'd add swooping, cave-dwelling bats, which strike terror into many people including my otherwise rational brother.)

Another explanation for dragons? The same fabulous discoveries that inspired this book: FOSSILS! People have been finding the stony remains of prehistoric giant animals for thousands of years. The Jurassic Coast of southwest England, for instance, is famous for its fossils of marine reptiles that erode from shoreline cliffs. It's not surprising that ancient people interpreted these and other remains in the form of terrifying, supersized dragons.

But not all dragons are scary. Some are the life of the party, like the Chinese dragon in a New Year's parade. Still, all dragons are powerful forces of nature, not to be trifled with — and they are timeless.

LEGENDS AND LORE

Fiery battles! Supernatural flights! Thunderous rainstorms, treacherous caves, and sparkling gems! Dragon adventures alone could fill this whole book. And still they would roar, "We want more pages!"

Many draconologists separate their favorite creature into two groups: benevolent Asian dragons and the fierce fire-breathers of the West. This division overlooks innumerable others, from the Rainbow Serpent of Australia to the dragon-like Nyami Nyami, said to dwell along Zambia's Zambezi River. To simplify, we'll define dragons as large flying creatures with bodies that combine features of many different animals, especially reptiles and fish. Most possess magical abilities related to weather. In the Philippines, for example, the legendary Bakunawa was said to cause eclipses, earthquakes, rain, and wind. (Oh, and it also enjoyed swallowing moons.)

Dragons play especially important roles in Chinese culture. For over five thousand years, the Chinese dragons, or *long* (龍), have symbolized power, good luck, and intelligence. Dragons are one of the Four Benevolent Animals in Chinese mythology and one of twelve animals of the zodiac. Ancient emperors claimed descent from dragons. Exuberant and joyful — sometimes wild and unruly — Chinese dragons also influenced mythologies of Japan, Korea, and other Asian cultures.

Western dragons can be traced to the ancient Near East, the region in Western Asia where many early civilizations arose. According to legends from four thousand years ago, an ocean serpent called Tiamat threatened to plunge the world into chaos. The young god Marduk saved the day by slaying the monster. Sound familiar? This long-ago tale is an early example of a popular plot about brave heroes battling the odds to defeat enormous, malevolent beasts.

Greek legends picked up on the theme. Zeus battled the giant serpent Typhon. Hercules slayed the nine-headed Hydra monster. The goddess Athena flung a dragon all the way up to the sky, where it became trapped among the stars. In northern Europe, an eighth-century epic poem told of Beowulf, a king who gave his life defeating a fire-spewing, treasure-hoarding dragon. (As Hobbit fans may know, J. R. R. Tolkien translated and taught *Beowulf* while he plotted the adventures of Bilbo Baggins.)

Western dragons took on more sinister roles as Christianity spread, reflecting their association with Satan according to the Bible's New Testament. Dragons were greedy, gluttonous, hungry for flesh — and believed to be part of the living world. Dragon-slaying reached a high point in the legends, artwork, and heraldry of medieval Europe. Those noble knights were busy! Belief in dragons faded as the natural world became better known. Yet the winged monsters continued to live on within stories of all kinds as vicious, evil-tempered beasts, always ready for a fight.

The dragon-like mušḫuššu of the Ishtar Gate (sixth century BCE) combines features of a lion, eagle, and snake. It symbolized Marduk, patron deity of ancient Babylon in modern-day Iraq.

The ouroboros is an ancient magical symbol of a serpent eating its tail. This Byzantine Greek drawing dates to around 1478. Much older versions were found in the Egyptian tomb of Tutankhamun (fourteenth century BCE).

The oldest recognizable image of a European dragon appeared in a bestiary from England around 1260 (**above**). Dragons were thought to be bearers of evil and special enemies of elephants.

In ancient Mesopotamian mythology the heroic Marduk battled the goddess Tiamat and created the heavens and the earth from her body (**below**). Tiamat reappeared as a multiheaded dragon in the popular role-playing game Dungeons & Dragons.

Fire-Breathers

Perched on a bridge in Ljubljana, Slovenia, this statue displays the characteristic batlike wings of European dragons. These ferocious, fire-spitting beasts typically had pointy stingers on their tails and skin covered with scaly armor. Most had four lionlike legs, but one version, the wyvern, had only two limbs. Some lived in caves and hoarded precious gems and gold. Dragon slayers aimed swords at the mouth—believed to be the creature's only weak spot—and hoped for the best.

George to the Rescue!

Among the most famous dragon hunters is Saint George, a Christian soldier credited with saving a princess from the jaws of a venom-spewing monster. The original story dates back to 315 CE, when a Roman officer fought a swamp creature (possibly a crocodile) in the North African country of Libya. Centuries later England adopted George as its patron saint.

Rain Bringers

Most Asian dragons flew by magic, with no need for wings. Others swam the seas. The Nine Dragon Screen in Beijing (1756) depicts dragons playing with pearls, which they often tucked under their chins. Chinese dragons typically had serpentine bodies and eagle-like claws. According to ancient texts, they had the heads of camels adorned with deer antlers and cow ears. Their glowing eyes were those of rabbits or demons, while the belly derived from crocodiles or clams. Colorful fish scales covered their bodies, and tiger paws formed the feet. Despite their scary appearance, Chinese dragons were well-disposed toward humans. They were not tame, however, and must be respected.

TRACKING DOWN CLUES

Snakes! Legless wonders. Masters of adaptation. Over the past one hundred million years, snakes have evolved a stunning array of survival strategies. Constrictors — like boas and pythons — use their bodies to hug prey to death. Venomous snakes, like cobras, inject neurotoxins through their fangs. Snakes inhabit a wide variety of habitats, too, from underground burrows to tropical seas.

Other big reptiles offer equally dazzling credentials of power and resilience. The saltwater crocodile is the largest living member, reaching lengths over twenty-three feet. With a few added details, like fire breath and wings, a crocodile could easily pass for a dragon.

You know what's even more impressive? PREHISTORIC reptiles. In a contest of biting power, the saltwater crocodile measures at sixteen thousand newtons (a measure of force). That's the strongest bite force of any living animal, but it's only half the estimated chomping ability of pliosaurs, giant marine reptiles from around one hundred million years ago. The top prize goes to *Tyrannosaurus rex*, the famous dinosaur that roamed North America from eighty-four to sixty-six million years ago. Its mighty jaws would have registered a whopping forty-five thousand newtons. (Our human jaws, by the way, exert a puny seven hundred newtons.)

Relax! We know that these terrifying creatures are extinct. Our ancestors, however, regarded fossils as proof of living, breathing monsters. In many parts of China, fossils are called "dragon bones." These remains have included many creatures over the centuries, but some were definitely dinosaurs. Ancient texts mention dragon bones from what is now the Sichuan Province, an area known for sedimentary rocks dating from the dinosaur era. Remains of meat-eating theropod dinos can be found there, along with massive sauropods with their extremely long necks.

Some ancient travelers linked specific fossils to legends. In the first century CE the Greek philosopher Apollonius heard tales of dragons during a journey through northern India. His route led through Himalayan foothills riddled with the fossils of animals that lived around five million years ago, from gigantic tortoises to shovel-tusked elephants. Some of the fossils contained large calcite crystals that formed as the animals' bones turned to stone. Local people hunted for these beautiful, iridescent crystals — the jewels, they claimed, of dragons.

Fossilized foot of a sauropod dinosaur.

The whole of India is girt with dragons of enormous size; for not only the marshes are full of them, but the mountains as well.

—Greek scholar Philostratus, in **Life of Apollonius**, c. 230 CE

Sea Dragons

While dinosaurs ruled the land, marine reptiles were terrorizing the waters of the Mesozoic Era (252 to 66 million years ago). Ichthyosaurs, plesiosaurs, and mosasaurs were streamlined, sharp-toothed predators. Some had dolphin-sized bodies, while others grew as long as good-sized whales. Mary Anning (**below right**) was only twelve years old when she and her brother found a huge ichthyosaur in the coastal cliffs of Lyme Regis, UK. Mary excavated more fossils through the early 1800s, like this pliosaur (**below left**) at London's Natural History Museum. Her discoveries helped to kickstart the science of paleontology.

An 1834 engraving by Felix Guerin depicts extinct animals based on fossil discoveries of the time.

Scaly Tales

Pythons and crocodiles (**right**) have long inhabited warm regions of Africa and Asia, making them possible influences on dragon folklore. Komodo dragons (**far right**) are the world's largest living lizards, growing up to ten feet long, with serrated teeth and venomous spit. Unknown to the Western world until 1912, they exist only on a few Indonesian islands today. Fossils of their ancient ancestors, however, have been discovered in Australia.

Terrible Lizards

Dinosaurs were named for Greek words meaning "terrible" and "lizard." These amazing reptiles were not actually lizards but part of the archosaur group along with crocodiles and pterosaurs. Through their long, 165-million-year history, dinosaurs left mega-sized fossils on all seven continents. In the current "golden age" of dinosaur discovery, roughly fifty new species are identified each year.

And dinosaurs are still with us. Experts like Dr. Jingmai O'Connor (**left**), a scientist at Chicago's Field Museum, are studying how some theropod dinosaurs evolved the power of flight—a trait used by most of the eleven thousand species of dinosaurs alive today (**birds**!). Dr. O'Connor conducts fieldwork in Spain, China, the United States, and many other countries. She and her team use high-resolution imaging to analyze fossilized bones and sometimes even the soft tissue of prehistoric animals.

This is the best time to be a paleontologist. New discoveries of fossils from around the world and new tools of investigation are rapidly transforming our understanding of extinct organisms.

—Dr. Jingmai Kathleen O'Connor, the "punk rock" paleontologist

TO BE A DRAGON

Hic eſt Draco *ille alatus et quadripes omni ævo memorabilis. quem Deodatus de Gozo Eques Hieroſolimitanus, in inſula Rhodo eo quo deſcripſimus ſtratagemate confecit. qui et ob beneficium in Inſulam collatum poſtmodum Magnus Ord. Magiſter Creatus eſt.*

Buckle your seat belt! We're taking on the power of flight.

In order to fly, a dragon needs to launch from the ground and travel through the air. Quick lesson on biomechanics: Powered flight involves four related forces. *Weight* is the force of gravity, which pulls the dragon down. *Lift* is the force that the dragon generates by creating differences in air pressure, such as by flapping its wings. This action offsets the dragon's weight and also contributes to *thrust*, the force that propels the dragon forward like an engine powers a plane. Finally, the force called *drag* pulls the dragon backward as air pushes against its body.

Given these factors, you can imagine that a light, strong, streamlined body makes it easier for an animal to fly. (Less weight and drag, more lift and thrust.) Which is great, because dragons — especially Chinese dragons — are serpentine and svelte. They don't have wings . . . but do they need them?

The flying snakes of Southeast Asia, for example, are wingless. To go airborne, a paradise tree snake launches itself from a branch. By flattening its body and wiggling in an S pattern, it can glide hundreds of feet. That twisting motion recalls the flowing character of some Asian dragons featured in artwork and dances.

But is the tree snake "flying"? Nope. It's gliding. Soon it will need to shimmy up another branch and start over. For powered flight an animal needs some kind of motor to generate lift. It needs wings! And like birds, it needs long, mostly hollow bones (imagine pulling on your arm and streeeeeetching it out). Add in powerful flight muscles and a supercharged breathing system, and our dragon is ready for liftoff.

Not so fast! Western dragons are huge, sturdy creatures. No offense to the adorable dragon pictured above, but those little bat wings won't be enough. Okay, how about bigger wings? The heaviest flying bird in Earth's history — Argentavis, an extinct bird of prey known from fossils in Argentina — weighed 150 pounds, with a twenty-foot wingspan. Impressive . . . but dragon-worthy?

Perhaps the best models for dragons are a group of extinct creatures we've already met — the pterosaurs, like *Quetzalcoatlus*. They didn't breathe fire, hoard treasure, or control the wind. But they're the largest flying animals of all time. The biggest grew to six hundred pounds, reaching the height of a giraffe and the wingspan of a small airplane. Some even grew elaborate crests on their head — perfect adornments for fabulous flying dragons.

Powered flight is about driving a blade-shaped limb through the air like a sword. If you make the air spin fast enough, it will hold you up!

—Dr. Michael Habib, *biomechanist and paleontologist*

The paradise tree snake of southeastern Asia measures about three feet long.

Chinese Dragon Alert

Dragons also love to swim! Chinese legends include dragons that inhabit water as well as air. A newly discovered, nearly complete fossil belongs to a twenty-foot-long reptile that inhabited the ancient sea of Tethys in what is now Guizhou Province, around 240 million years ago. The international team of paleontologists nicknamed it the "Chinese dragon" due to its remarkably long, snakelike neck. They announced the finding in February 2024, the beginning of the Year of the Dragon.

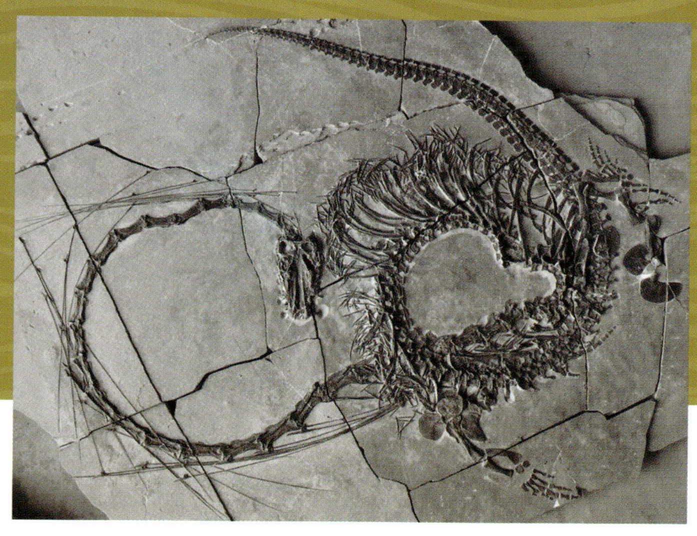

How to Fly: Advice from a Pterosaur Expert

Dr. Michael Habib had a question: How did pterosaurs launch themselves into the air? Did they jump off the edges of cliffs? Did they run really fast to build up speed, like an airplane on a runway? Did the big guys, like **Quetzalcoatlus**, even fly at all? And why did some pterosaurs get so much bigger than any flying birds?

Combining his skills in biodynamics, paleontology, and art, Dr. Habib considered the pterosaur's bizarre-looking anatomy. Their bodies were front-loaded, with long necks and massive heads and chests. Their leathery, sail-like wings extended from their ankles to their extremely long fourth fingers. When the animals landed, they folded their wings back and walked on all four limbs.

Could that be a clue? Birds are bipedal, walking upright on two hind legs. To fly they use those back legs to launch themselves and then flap their wings. From a mechanical perspective this means that birds use separate "motors" for launching (legs) and flying (wings). Once they're aloft, the back motor doesn't help them—it's extra baggage.

Pterosaurs evolved a different strategy for powered flight. Because their front legs touched the ground, pterosaurs could use all four limbs to make a standing jump. That means they had two motors for liftoff, both firing at the same time. Pterosaur superpower! Dr. Habib tested the idea with special equipment to look inside the fossil bones of pterosaurs. This careful work confirmed that pterosaurs employed both front and back limbs to launch. Such high-powered takeoffs would provide enough clearance for even the largest pterosaurs to start flapping their wings. Once airborne they could capture the wind . . . and soar.

Mini-Dragons

The Draco lizards of Southeast Asia could teach an aspiring dragon a few tricks. These eight-inch-long "flying dragons" move around the forest by gliding between trees, which helps them avoid predators. When it launches from a branch, a Draco lizard unfurls winglike folds of skin, supported by extended ribs on its sides. Then it reaches back and grabs the wings with its front feet. This enables the lizard to steer and do barrel-roll maneuvers as it travels over one hundred feet in a single leap. Not bad for a little guy!

Dragons are fire and air, water and earth. They are snakes and lions, eagles and fish. We revere them, fear them, and long to fly perched on their backs. They remind us of long-lost monsters that live only as stone-hard fossils today — and their glittering treasures are the stories that we tell, retell, and create anew.

Long live the dragons!

MAKE SOME GOOD MONSTERS

We share the world with millions of animals. Many, many others have left their fossils behind. Long ago some of those creatures made their ways into myths about giant beasts, tiny fairies, and elusive spirits of ocean and stream. To our ancestors these stories explained the workings of the world.

And what wonderful stories they are!

Today we dig fossils from the earth, adding missing pieces to the puzzle of life. We study wildlife and understand how animal populations evolve, survive, and go extinct. We share cultural traditions in many forms of media — yet ancient myths endure. We return to them, over and over, for inspiration and delight.

This book describes only a few of many mythical beings from cultures around the world. None of these creatures emerged fully formed from one particular time or place. They changed through generations, taking on different meanings and roles. They are important to many traditions today.

What new stories will you create? Whether you're writing or drawing or making a game — have fun. Do your research. Be brave. Build marvelous worlds.

Bring the old legends to life . . . and make some new ones.

Artist Júlia d'Oliveira created this rendering of **Mamenchisaurus sinocanadorum**, a type of sauropod dinosaur that lived around 160 million years ago. Their fossils, discovered in northwest China, suggest that these amazing animals had necks up to fifty feet long (that's ten feet longer than a typical school bus!).

Ammonites were marine animals that left spiral-shaped fossils around the world. In British folklore ammonites were believed to be snakes that had turned to stone, earning them the name "snakestones." Some people carved heads on the fossils, like this one named in honor of Saint Hilda in 1789.

Dragons, unicorns, and other mythical beasts hold the power to spark imagination and inspire journeys of curiosity and scientific discovery. They may only exist in our dreams, yet they play important roles in our world.

—Gabriel-Philip Santos, paleontologist and founder of Cosplay for Science

Dragons of water and sky at Foshan Ancestor Temple in Foshan, China.

AUTHOR'S NOTE

Ten years ago, I spotted a dusty old book at a library sale called *Mermaids and Mastodons: A Book of Natural & Unnatural History* by Richard Carrington. When I opened the cover, a shiver ran up my spine. Fossils, dragons, ancient art . . . how could I resist?

Dinosaurs to Dragons began in that moment. The project changed me as a person, expanding my horizons to new places, cultures, and natural wonders. Despite that long and thrilling journey, however, I know that this book barely scratches the surface of mythical traditions around the world. I hope that it does so in a respectful manner and that readers will travel far beyond these pages to discover more.

ACKNOWLEDGMENTS

I am deeply grateful to three advisors who guided this book from start to finish.

- **Adrienne Mayor**, research scholar, author, and historian of ancient science. Thank you for your pioneering work and advice, including wise reminders that we can never pinpoint the true beginnings of a legend.
- **Dr. Joshua H. Miller**, Associate Professor of Geosciences at the University of Cincinnati; research associate of the Smithsonian National Museum of Natural History and University of Alaska Museum of the North. Thank you for ideas and corrections that vastly improved the discussions of science in this book.
- **Gabriel-Philip Santos**, Raymond M. Alf Museum of Paleontology; cohost, *PBS Eons*; cofounder, Cosplay for Science. Thanks, Gabe, for helping me to balance fantasy, science, and critical thinking throughout these pages.

In addition, I am indebted to many experts who reviewed specific chapters and topics. I apologize for any inadvertent omissions.

Ms. Tonya Abari, Consultant; **Dr. Persephone Braham**, Department of Languages, Literatures and Cultures, University of Delaware; **Dr. Dorothy Bray**, Department of English, McGill University; **Dr. Julia Clarke**, Department of Geosciences, University of Texas, Austin; **Dr. Philip A. Clarke**, Anthropologist, South Australian Museum; **Dr. Rory Cooper**, Developmental biologist, University of Sheffield; **Dr. Todd Disotell**, Department of Anthropology, University of Massachusetts, Amherst; **Dr. Nick Fraser**, Keeper of Natural Sciences, National Museums Scotland; **Dr. Michael Habib**, Paleontologist and biomechanist, Natural History Museum of Los Angeles and University of California, Los Angeles; **Mr. Mark Koolmatrie**, Ngarrindjeri Elder, Adelaide, Australia; **Ms. Ye Luo**, Design professional and native of Hunan, China; **Dr. Charlotte Lindqvist**, Department of Biological Sciences, University at Buffalo; **Ms. Marianne McShane**, Librarian and author, Ireland; **Dr. Patrick Nunn**, Department of Geography, University of the Sunshine Coast, Australia; **Dr. Jingmai O'Connor**, Associate Curator of Fossil Reptiles, Field Museum, Chicago and adjunct professor, Chinese Academy of Sciences, Beijing, China; **Mr. Owen Oliver**, Writer, artist, and member of the Quinault Indian Nation; **Dr. Lauren Poyer**, Department of Scandinavian Studies, University of Washington; **Mr. Benjamin Radford**, Deputy Editor, Skeptical Inquirer science magazine; **Dr. Patricia Rich**, School of Earth, Atmosphere and Environment, Monash University, Australia; **Dr. Richard "Bert" Roberts**, Faculty of Science, University of Wollongong, Australia; **Dr. Daniel C. Taylor**, Conservationist, Future Generations University; **Dr. Bertina Olmedo Vera**, Curator of Mexican Collections, Museo Nacional de Antropología, Mexico City, Mexico; and **Dr. Edith Widder**, Cofounder, Ocean Research & Conservation Association.

Heartfelt appreciation to my writer friends for sharpening each clumsy draft, especially Alexandria Giardino, Amy Butler Greenfield, Linda Elovitz Marshall, and Susanna Reich. Big hugs to superhero agent Ammi-Joan Paquette, who never gave up on D2D. Many thanks to our beloved *consuegros*, Karina Rivas and Carlos Sanchez, for revealing the ancient wonders of Mexico City, to Caroline Lawrence for an insider tour of the British Museum, and to the master detectives of image licensing at Photo Affairs, Danny Meldung and Steve Rouben. As always, much love to my darling muse and traveling companion, Ken Robinson, and to our three sons, whose childhood fascinations with fantasy creatures inspired me to write.

And to the team: Giant, kraken-sized thanks to Julia McCarthy, who edited this book with her own special blend of whimsy and common sense; to Violeta Encarnación for gorgeous artwork; and to Michael McCartney, Anum Shafqat, Kaitlyn San Miguel, and everyone at Atheneum who conjured *Dinosaurs to Dragons* to life. You are truly magical.

GLOSSARY

Archaeologists study ancient civilizations by excavating and analyzing the structures, landscapes, and objects (pottery, tools, or other artifacts) left by past cultures.

BCE stands for "Before the Common Era." It is used for dates that precede year CE 1 of the world's commonly used (Gregorian) calendar. An alternative abbreviation is BC, for "Before Christ."

CE stands for "Common Era," the time period beginning in year CE 1. An alternative abbreviation is AD, for the Latin expression *Anno Domini*, meaning "in the year of the Lord."

Deities are gods, goddesses, or other supernatural beings.

Evolution is the process by which life-forms adapt and change over time in response to their environments.

Folklore comprises the traditional stories, customs, and beliefs of a culture, usually passed down through the generations by word of mouth and often not set in the real world.

Fossils are preserved traces of prehistoric life, typically older than 10,000 years. Body fossils are the remains of an organism, such as bones that become mineralized. Trace fossils include footprints, burrows, imprints of leaves or shells, or preserved dung called *coprolite*.

Historians collect and study information about human events, often using original text or pictorial sources from long ago.

Humanoid creatures are not human but show similar characteristics, such as upright, bipedal walking and bodies with two arms, two legs, and a head.

Ice ages are periods of time when large parts of the Earth were covered in ice. The last major Ice Age ended around 11,000 years ago.

Legends are ancient tales that feature human actions, usually set in the real world. Legends are often regarded as historical events yet cannot be proven.

Medieval times refer to the period of European history from the fifth century to the fifteenth century, also known as the **Middle Ages**.

Myths are traditional sacred stories about gods, heroes, or supernatural creatures that explain important questions, such as how the world came to be.

Philosophers of ancient times were scholars who studied and taught a wide range of topics, from ethics to the workings of the natural world. They often served as advisors to rulers.

Scientists are people who systematically gather and use evidence to understand how the world works. Scientists specialize in different topics: **Biologists** study living organisms and systems, while **geologists** study Earth's structure, composition, and history. **Paleontologists** explore fossils and other evidence of prehistoric life. **Zoologists** study living animals and their habitats.

Species refers to a group of organisms with similar characteristics that can interbreed and produce healthy, fertile offspring.

SELECTED SOURCES

Research for *Dinosaurs to Dragons* drew from a wide range of books, articles, interviews, and websites. Here is a small sampling of books; for a full bibliography please visit www.elizabethshreeve.com.

Arnold, Martin. *The Dragon: Fear and Power.* Reaktion Books, 2018.

Bainbridge, David. *Paleontology: An Illustrated History.* Princeton University Press, 2022.

Briggs, Katharine. *An Encyclopedia of Fairies.* Pantheon, 1978.

Cahir, Fred, Ian D. Clark, and Philip A. Clarke. *Aboriginal Biocultural Knowledge in South-eastern Australia.* Csiro Publishing, 2018.

Carrington, Richard. *Mermaids and Mastodons: A Book of Natural & Unnatural History.* Rinehart, 1957.

Cunliffe, Barry. *The Scythians: Nomad Warriors of the Steppe.* Oxford University Press, 2019.

Curley, Michael J., trans. *Physiologus: A Medieval Book of Nature Lore.* University of Chicago Press, 2009.

Delacampagne, Ariane, and Christian Delacompagne. *Here Be Dragons: A Fantastic Bestiary.* Princeton University Press, 2003.

Drewal, Henry John, ed. *Sacred Waters: Arts for Mami Wata and Other Divinities in Africa and the Diaspora.* Indiana University Press, 2008.

Holden, Robert, and Nicholas Holden. *Bunyips: Australia's Folklore of Fear*. National Library of Australia, 2001.

Kendall, Laurel, Mark A. Norell, and Richard Ellis. *Mythic Creatures: And the Impossibly Real Animals Who Inspired Them*. Sterling Signature, 2016.

Loxton, Daniel, and Donald R. Prothero. *Abominable Science! Origins of the Yeti, Nessie, and Other Famous Cryptids*. Columbia University Press, 2013.

Mayor, Adrienne. *Flying Snakes and Griffin Claws: And Other Classical Myths, Historical Oddities, and Scientific Curiosities*. Princeton University Press, 2022.

Mayor, Adrienne. *Fossil Legends of the First Americans*. Princeton University Press, 2005.

Mayor, Adrienne. *The Amazons: Lives & Legends of Warrior Women Across the Ancient World*. Princeton University Press, 2016.

Mayor, Adrienne. *The First Fossil Hunters: Dinosaurs, Mammoths, and Myth in Greek and Roman Times*. Princeton University Press, 2011.

McNamara, Ken. *Dragons' Teeth and Thunderstones: The Quest for the Meaning of Fossils*. Reaktion Books, 2020.

Nigg, Joseph. *Sea Monsters: The Lore and Legacy of Olaus Magnus' Marine Map*. Ivy Press, 2013.

Nigg, Joseph. *The Phoenix: An Unnatural Biography of a Mythical Beast*. University of Chicago Press, 2016.

Nigg, Joe. *Wonder Beasts: Tales and Lore of the Phoenix, the Griffin, the Unicorn, and the Dragon*. Libraries Unlimited, 1995.

Novato, Ernesto. *Quetzalcoatl: The History and Legacy of the Feathered Serpent God in Mesoamerican Mythology*. Charles River Editors, 2022.

Nunn, Patrick. *The Edge of Memory: Ancient Stories, Oral Tradition and the Post-Glacial World*. Bloomsbury Sigma, 2018.

Sax, Boria. *Dinomania: Why We Love, Fear and Are Utterly Enchanted by Dinosaurs*. Reaktion Books, 2018.

Sax, Boris. *Imaginary Animals: The Monstrous, the Wondrous and the Human*. Reaktion Books, 2013.

Shepard, Odell. *The Lore of the Unicorn*. New York: HarperCollins, 1979.

Sugg, Richard. *Fairies: A Dangerous History*. Reaktion Books, 2018.

Taylor, Daniel C. *Yeti: The Ecology of a Mystery*. Oxford University Press, 2017.

Widder, Edith. *Below the Edge of Darkness: A Memoir of Exploring Light and Life in the Deep Sea*. Random House, 2021.

Williams, Wendy. *Kraken: The Curious, Exciting, and Slightly Disturbing Science of Squid*. Abrams, 2011.

IMAGE CREDITS

LEGEND: *L* = left, *R* = right, *T* = top, *B* = bottom, *C* = center

GRIFFIN: 3*T* Album/Alamy; 3*B* 24.97.51/Metropolitan Museum of Art; 5*T* 2002.482.9/Metropolitan Museum of Art; 5*B* Heritage Images/Getty; 7*T&B* American Museum of Natural History; 7*C* Ivan Vdovin/Alamy; 8*T* Brooklyn Museum, Charles Edwin Wilbour Fund, 53.173; 8*B* MCLA/Alamy; 9*T* Zev Radovan/Alamy; 9*B* Ana Lo/Shutterstock.

UNICORN: 11*TL* North Wind/Alamy; 11*TR* Niday/Alamy; 11*R* Spencer Museum of Art, University of Kansas, Gift of Mr. and Mrs. Forrest E. Jones, 1950.0092; 12 Science History Images/Alamy; 13*TL* Purchase from the J. H. Wade Fund 1973.161/Cleveland Museum of Art; 13*TR* CPA Media Pte Ltd/Alamy; 13*L* Walters Art Museum, Baltimore; 13*C* 91.1.965/Metropolitan Museum of Art; 13*R* Mondadori Portfolio/Getty; 13*BL* Norweb Collection 1963.678/Cleveland Museum of Art; 13*BR* Chris Dorney/Alamy; 14 Agustin Diaz; 15*TL* Ivan Vdovin/Alamy; 15*TC* Sven Sachs; 15*TR* Keenan Taylor; 15*B* Dave Pape, University at Buffalo; 16 Malcolm J. Brenner, Eyes Open Media; 17*L* 37.80.6/Metropolitan Museum of Art; 17*R* Photo 12/Alamy.

YETI: 19 Artist, Tashi Lama. Used by Permission; 20 Ed Vebell/Getty Images; 21*TL* Melissa Jooste/Alamy; 21*CR* Danny Ye/Alamy; 21*CL* Ray Troll; 21*BL* Marion Kaplan/Alamy; 21*BR* © Canada Post Corporation, 1990/© Société canadienne des postes, 1990. Reproduced with Permission; 22 PA Images/Alamy; 23*TR* Dave Stamboulis/Alamy; 23*CR* Nobuo Matsumura/Alamy; 23*BL* John Sibbick/Science Source; 24 Archives Charmet/Bridgeman; 25*L* Maayan Harel; 25*R* Andrew Wrighting/Alamy.

BUNYIP: 27*BL* Benny Marty/Alamy; 27*BR* Greg C Grace/Alamy; 28 History and Art Collection/Alamy; 29*TL* History Collection/Alamy; 29*TR* Ron Brooks; 29*C* ARTGEN/Alamy; 29*B* © Trustees of the British Museum. All rights reserved; 30 & 31*TR* Stocktrek Images/Alamy; 31*TL* Hi-Story/Alamy; 31*BL* John Carnemolla/Shutterstock; 31*BR* Imogen Warren, CC BY-SA 4.0; 32*T* Chau Chak Wing Museum, University of Sydney, NHM.45.2; 32*B* Philosophical Transactions of the Royal Society of London, v. 1870, Part 2. Pl. XXXV; 33*T* Ashley Cooper/Alamy; 33*B* Artwork by Peter Trusler, © Australia Post 2008.

MERMAID: 35*TR* & 36 steeve-x-art/Alamy; 35*B* Frantz Zéphirin; 37(Lasirèn) Courtesy of the artist Myrland

Constant and Fort Gansevoort, New York; 37 (Ningyo) Hansrad Collection/Alamy; 37 (Etruscan Sea-Girl) Peter Horree/Alamy; 37 (Mermaid of Mexico) © Trustees of the British Museum. All rights reserved; 37 (Ceasg, Maid of the Wave) Stamp design © Royal Mail Group Limited; 37 (Sedna) © Canada Post Corporation, 1980/© Société canadienne des postes, 1980. Reproduced with permission; 37 (Yawkyawk) Art Directors & TRIP/Alamy; 38*L* Ian Bottle/Alamy; 38*R* © Trustees of the British Museum. All rights reserved; 39*TL* NPL/Alamy; 39*C* Signal Photos/Alamy; 39*BL* JJ Harrison, CC BY-SA 3.0; 40*T* Justine Evans/Alamy; 40*B* State Archives of Florida; 41*R* Popperfoto/Getty; 41*L* Arterra/Alamy.

KRAKEN: 43*TR* Herbert Kawainui Kāne; 43*BL* Lakeview Images/Alamy; 45*T* Science History Images/Alamy; 45*L* *Vingt mille lieues sous les mers* by J. Verne, 1871, p. 400; 45*R* Typ 620.22.697. Houghton Library, Harvard University; 45*BR* Picture Art Collection/Alamy; 47*T* Edith Widder; 47*CR* Dive Resort T-Style (www.takeno-diving.com); 47*BL* Free Library of Philadelphia; 47*BR* G. Loates; 48*T* Chronicle/Alamy; 48*B* sciencepics/Shutterstock; 49*T* Timewatch Images/Alamy; 49*B* North Wind/Alamy.

FAIRIES: 51*C* Charles Walker Collection/Alamy; 51*B* Boston Public Library, Norman B. Leventhal Map & Education Center, G9930 1917 .S51; 52 & 53*TL* Science History Images/Alamy; 53*TR* ART Collection/Alamy; 53*CL* *The brownies and other tales* by J.H.G. Ewing, 1910; 53*CR* Godo; 53*BL* Dundee Art Galleries and Museums/Bridgeman; 53*BR* © Trustees of the British Museum. All rights reserved; 54*L* Medici/Mary Evans; 54*R* NYPL Digital Collections, 1875, no. 1699736; 55*T* Arthur Ruffino/Alamy; 55*B* Image © National Museums Scotland; 56*T* Bogon, K./Alamy; 56*C* Library Book Collection/Alamy; 56*B* Kevin Schafer/Alamy; 57*T* *Coming of the fairies* by A.C. Doyle, 1922. p. 48; 57*B* *Celtic fairy tales* by J. Jacobs, 1892. p. 26; 57C (fairy house) Photo by author.

PHOENIX: 59*TR* NASA; 59*C* © Trustees of the British Museum. All rights reserved; 59*BL* NPL/DeA/Bridgeman; 59*BR* 17.9.1/Metropolitan Museum of Art; 60*BL* © Trustees of the British Museum. All rights reserved; 60*BR* IanDagnall/Alamy; 61*T* Juniors Bildarchiv/Alamy; 61*BL* Mary Evans; 61*BC* Artepics/Alamy; 61*BR* Historic Images/Alamy; 62*L* Dr. Paula Sanders, Rice University; 62*C* Terence Waeland/Alamy; 62*R* Varesvuo, M./Alamy; 62*BL* *Nouveau recueil de planches coloriées d'oiseaux* by C.J. Temminck, 1838, p. 474; 62*BR* Jeff Dahl, CC BY-SA 4.0; 63*T* Lanmas/Alamy; 63*BL* Picture Art Collection/Alamy; 63*BC* NPL/DeA/Bridgeman; 63*BR* World History Archive/Alamy; 64 British Library/Bridgeman; 65*TL* Adisha Pramod/Alamy; 65*C* Mauricio Anton/Science Source; 65*R* Photo by author; 65*BL* A. Dagli Orti/NPL/DeA/Bridgeman.

QUETZALCOATL: 67*TL* Valentine De Liscia/Hyperallergenic; 67*B* Photos by author; 68 imageBROKER/Alamy; 69*TL* IanDagnall/Alamy; 69*TR* Picture Art Collection/Alamy; 69*CL* Igor Kisselev/Alamy; 69*CR* © Trustees of the British Museum. All rights reserved; 69B Panther Media/Alamy; 70*L* Thomas Chamberlin/Alamy; 70*C* imageBROKER/Alamy; 70*R* Photo by author; 71*T* Volker Preusser/Alamy; 71*CL* LOC/Jay I. Kislak/Science Source; 71*CR* Photo by author; 71*B* John Mitchell/Alamy; 72 SJArt/Alamy; 73*T* Mark Turner/Alamy; 73*R* PhotoEdit/Alamy; 73*B* © Trustees of the British Museum. All rights reserved.

DRAGONS: 75*T* CPA Media Pte Ltd/Alamy; 75*B* 1999.263a, b/Metropolitan Museum of Art; 76*L* VPC Travel Photo/Alamy; 76*R* Picture Art Collection/Alamy; 77*TL* History Collection/Alamy; 77*TR* freeartist/Alamy; 77*C* NYPL Digital Collections, 1853, no. 494724; 77*BL* Lebrecht/Alamy; 77*BR* Charles Walker Collection/Alamy; 78*L* Corbin17/Alamy; 78*C* Sergio Azenha/Alamy; 78*R* CBW/Alamy; 79*TL* Florilegius/Alamy; 79*TC* Roberto Nistri/Alamy; 79*TR* NPL/Alamy; 79*CR* GFC Collection/Alamy; 79*BL* Jochen Stierberger; 80*T* INTERFOTO/Alamy; 80*B* blickwinkel/Alamy; 81*T* Image © National Museums Scotland; 81*C* UIG/Alamy; 81*B* Jason Wells/Alamy.

MAKE SOME GOOD MONSTERS: 82 MCLA/Alamy; 83*R* Júlia d'Oliveira; 83*L* Natural History Museum/Alamy; 83*B* maximimages/Alamy.

TEXT CREDIT: 29 "The Bunyip" from *My People, 5th Edition* by Oodgeroo Noonuccal, October 2020, p. 71. Used by permission of John Wiley & Sons, Inc.